"WHATEVER HAPPENED
TO THE GOOD NEWS?"

"Whatever happened to the *GOOD* News?"

Niall Walshe

The Pentland Press Limited
Edinburgh · Cambridge · Durham · USA

All Biblical references, unless otherwise stated,
are from the Holy Bible New International Version
Copyright © 1973 1978 1984 by International Bible Society.

© Niall Walshe 2001

First published in 2001 by
The Pentland Press Ltd.
1 Hutton Close
South Church
Bishop Auckland
Durham

All rights reserved.
Unauthorised duplication
contravenes existing laws.

British Library Cataloguing in Publication Data.
A catalogue record for this book is available
from the British Library.

ISBN 1 85821 836 5

Typeset by George Wishart & Associates, Whitley Bay.
Printed and bound by Antony Rowe Ltd., Chippenham

Contents

Foreword	....	vii
Introduction	....	xi

Part one – The doctrine of grace

Chapter 1	An introduction to grace	....	1
Chapter 2	Secure in grace	....	11
Chapter 3	Grace: easy option or source of power?	....	23
Chapter 4	Jesus' grace parables	....	35
Chapter 5	Grace Scriptures	....	52

Part two – More Christian doctrine

Chapter 6	'Repent and believe . . .'	....	65
Chapter 7	The Commandments and the Christian	....	83
Chapter 8	Forgiveness	....	104
Chapter 9	Obedience	....	119
Chapter 10	Righteousness	....	136

Part three – More *Good* News

Chapter 11	Some very ordinary people	....	151
Chapter 12	The Believer in Christ	....	166
Chapter 13	'. . . as of first importance . . .'	....	171

Foreword

In his book 'Mere Christianity,' C.S. Lewis recorded this statement about God, 'We know that if there does exist an absolute goodness, it must detest most what we do. That is a terrible fix we are in. If the universe is not governed by an absolute goodness, then all our efforts in the long run are hopeless. But if it is then we are making ourselves enemies of that goodness every day; and are not in the least likely to do any better tomorrow, and so our case is hopeless again. We cannot do without it and we cannot do with it. God is the only comforter; He is also the supreme terror; the thing we need most and the thing we most want to hide from. He is our only possible ally, and we have made ourselves His enemies.'

In all the years of seeking, I have found this statement to be true. All of us fall short of His glorious standard and none of us deserves His acceptance. God has, however, provided a way out of this dilemma for us, and that way is grace.

A number of years ago, when a group of us were learning to counsel, a lovely Christian lady told us of a man who had come to her for help. He wanted very much to accept God's offer of love and become a Believer, but he had a terrible secret in his past. He had murdered a young child, and had managed to get away without being discovered. Now that he was coming face to face with God, this terrible secret was burning within him. He wondered if it would be right by God to turn himself over to the authorities, admit what he had done and accept the consequences. I want you to imagine that this man did hand himself over to the authorities. He was tried, convicted and sentenced to die. Imagine that whilst he was on Death Row, the father of the small murdered child came to speak to the prison authorities. His request? He wanted the prison authorities to allow the convicted murderer to come home with him, live with him and become a member of his family, whilst the father would send his own son to prison – with the son's willing agreement – to die in the murderer's place. Such a scene may be beyond the understanding of human beings, but it illustrates what God has done for mankind. Jesus Christ bore the punishment for man's sins on Calvary's cross to set us free from them. The innocent paid the price for the guilty. God sent His Son to die so that we could become His children. Grace is that matchless and magnificent. It is at once too good to be true, and yet so good that it can only be true. It is a completely free gift from God. Grace is not about what we deserve, it is about God not counting our sins against us.

The problem today is that the Church has largely misunderstood this amazing grace. In Jesus' day people such as the murderer described earlier ran towards Jesus – not away from Him. Although He was the most morally upright man that lived, sinners adored Him – the tax collectors, a prostitute who interrupted a dinner, a wicked woman at a well, a dying thief who would never make restitution for what he had done. Such people saw Jesus in much the same way as C.S. Lewis did – possibly their supreme terror but, also, their only hope. Jesus is still our only hope today.

I have known Niall Walshe for many years. We met around the time that he began his search for God. Over the years we have managed to maintain a friendship despite the 5,000 miles between us. Niall has become Godparent to my three children – Kimberley, Robin and Timothy – and despite the great distance, he manages to visit them regularly. The main reason for our friendship being sustained is that we have been fellow-travellers along this path of seeking after God's grace. Niall has always been seeking after those 'pearls of great price' hidden in the fields of God's Word and has truly found the best one of all. The search has been all-out and long and the path has been studded with many difficulties and heartbreaks, many blessings and victories. This search has culminated in the writing of this book, which, having had a preview of the material, I can thoroughly recommend. We have already used some of this material and seen people being set free as God's grace has done its work in people's lives. I never grow tired of seeing people's faces light up as they begin to realize what

FOREWORD

God's grace is all about and its truth begins to penetrate into the deep levels of their lives.

In the Book of Acts Paul commends the Bereans for checking all his teachings against Scriptures, and I know that Niall would also want readers to do likewise. It is imperative that we check these things for ourselves to make sure that our foundation in Christ is absolutely rock-solid.

I would like to thank Niall very much for taking the time and making the effort to put his search for God into a book so that many other people can benefit. My prayer is that God will use it to make a change in many lives. May the Lord continue to bless you, Niall.

Carol Tucker
Tengwe, Zimbabwe
June 2000

Introduction

Background to the book

Jesus entered a society in which the church of His time was responsible for the leading astray of multitudes of Believers. He took the church to task for this. Endless times in the Gospels it can be seen that Jesus' greatest battles were with the leadership of the church, the Pharisees, Sadducees and the teachers of the Law. He frankly warned His followers, 'Be on your guard against the yeast of the Pharisees and the Sadducees. Then they understood that He was not telling them to guard against the yeast used in bread, but against the teaching of the Pharisees and Sadducees' (Matt. 16:11-12).

Between 1988 and 1999 I worked among the homeless youngsters living on the streets of London. As well as working on the streets, I ran two short stay accommodation units and one longer stay unit and, also, a drop-in coffee bar. Over those years I was greatly blessed in seeing many of the homeless youngsters come into a very real faith in Jesus Christ. I saw also that this living faith did not necessarily, for whatever reason, empower them to overcome the crippling damage that many had suffered as children – abuse in all its forms and extremes. This left some if not many of them still struggling, but now as Christians, with drugs, drink, lack of self-worth and a host of other life-controlling problems.

These problems were added to by a church that did not accept these struggling young brothers and sisters. These youngsters received a message, over and over again, that said, 'When you are doing well, you are welcome; but when you are back on drugs, on drink or in trouble with the Police then you are not so welcome.' Many times over the years I became very angry at a church which, instead of embracing the outcast, rejected them in the same way they had been rejected all their lives. There were, of course, various wonderful Christians who did not respond in this way; but the majority did.

However, I came to realize that the church people were not really to blame. They, like the homeless youngsters, were also victims of their backgrounds. In the case of the Christian churchgoer their background, in church, consisted of teaching which was mirrored in their attitude to the homeless. In other words they received endless teaching which essentially taught them that God loves and blesses them more when they are making lots of effort and living 'a good Christian life.' They were only passing on to the homeless youngsters what they understood to be God's approach and attitude to them.

I came to see that the majority of the church is living with a confused, and confusing, mixture of Old and New Covenant teachings. So many messages, so many books, so much teaching points the Christian back to himself, his effort and what he is doing for God. Christians, as a church, are back with an Old Covenant style relationship with God. Hence the church's inability to accept a young brother who still needed drugs to cope with each day or a young sister who gave herself into a physical relationship in order to feel needed and loved.

It became my heart's desire to write a book which brought out the simple, glorious truths of the Good News. So much church teaching is now a blurred mixture of good and bad news, a mixture of salvation by grace and salvation by works. It is apparent that many of the teachers of the faith, as in Jesus' day, are proving to be more of a hindrance than a help. This is not malicious on their part, but merely through their own confusion about the fundamental truths of our faith. Jesus Christ loves the church. He refers to it as His bride. Christians, for the sake of Christ, should love the church that He loves – even with all its imperfections. That love of church will sometimes lead to a need to confront error – as Paul confronted Peter, in Galatians 2, when Peter slipped back into an Old Covenant approach to the Gentiles. This book is an attempt to reaffirm for the church, and the non-Christian, the Good News that God, through Jesus, gave to mankind.

PART ONE – **THE DOCTRINE OF GRACE**

CHAPTER 1

An introduction to grace

The common Christian experience

A lot of Scriptures, readily quoted, remain a complete unreality for the very Christians who quote them. For example: Romans 5:1 'Therefore, since we have been justified through faith, we have *peace with God* through our Lord Jesus Christ,' (author's emphasis). Romans 8:1 'Therefore, there is *'now no condemnation* for those who are in Christ Jesus,' (author's emphasis). These are not Scriptures attainable only by those with great faith. These are to do with the absolute basics of the Christian faith. Yet for many Christians the Scriptures just quoted, and many others like them, are a complete nonsense. For many Christians these Scriptures, although the Word of God, simply do not represent reality because for many there is **no peace** with God, for many **there is condemnation**.

It is not unusual to find Christians struggling with a sense of unworthiness, to find Christians who believe that they are not very good Christians, that they aren't doing very much for God, that God probably doesn't love them very much. It is quite common to find Christians who are burdened by a sense of failure, of guilt and of condemnation.

It is very common to find Christians who are on a merry-go-round of apparently failing, striving to do better, failing again, striving again – an endless cycle. Sadly, it is not uncommon to find Christians who have given up any attempt to live the Christian life. Some Believers feel they will simply never 'make the grade' and the effort of trying has brought them too much unhappiness to make it worthwhile continuing.

The Church needs to be re-focused onto God's grace and truth – as revealed in and by Jesus Christ. One young Christian man, who had been homeless and was struggling to be free of the curse of drugs, discovered this truth and wrote, 'I have been looking at my life lately and feeling very depressed. I need to be continually pointed to Jesus, for when I am there is so much joy, peace and strength to serve.' Such is the power of the Gospel of Christ, the grace of God.

What is grace?

A well known expression reveals grace as ***God's Riches At Christ's Expense***. A simple expression; yet it does accurately explain grace. The Believer has laid before him or her the very riches of God – '. . . every spiritual blessing in Christ' (Eph. 1:3). What is Christ's is also the Believer's. That which God has, in His mercy, chosen to bestow upon every Believer is not free. There is an enormous price tag attached to the exalted position within which the Believer finds himself – 'And God raised us up with Christ and seated us with Him in the heavenly realms in Christ Jesus' (Eph. 2:6). The Good News of the Gospel is that Jesus Christ has paid the price – **in full**! God the Father is now free to pour out, into the lives of Believers, the unlimited love and blessings that He has for each and every Christian. The limitless love and blessings of Almighty God are available because Jesus Christ paid the price for the sinfulness of each Believer. Or, put another way, **God's Riches At Christ's Expense**.

Some reasons for understanding grace

The Scriptures give very good reasons why it is so important that every Believer has a clear understanding of grace. For many there is an understanding that grace is an easy option, that it is an alternative to obedience; yet the Scriptures reveal the very opposite. Romans 5:1-2 says, 'Therefore since we have been justified through faith, we have peace with God through our Lord Jesus Christ, through whom we have gained access by faith into this grace in which we now stand.' *It is grace which enables the Believer to stand.* 1 Peter 5:12 makes the same point when Peter

AN INTRODUCTION TO GRACE

writes about what he terms, '... the true grace of God' and then urges his readers to, 'stand fast in it.' Christians who are struggling to stand, in whatever way within their Christian life, should take hold of God's grace and stand strong in it. Repeatedly it will be seen in Scripture that grace is the very source of power and obedience in the life of a Christian, and it is for that reason that the truth of grace must be grasped. Romans 5:17 is a verse of great promise on the power of grace to transform the life of any Believer who is struggling in any area of their life; it says, '... how much more will those who receive God's abundant provision of grace and of the gift of righteousness reign in life through the one man, Jesus Christ.' Here is a two-fold promise: firstly, that God's grace is provided in abundance – which the dictionary defines as being 'more than enough' – and the second powerful promise of this verse is that whoever receives this abundant grace will reign in life. There are those who might point the Christian to greater effort, self-discipline and determination as the way of overcoming unchristian ways in the life of a Believer; *the Bible points the Believer to God's grace as the means by which the Christian overcomes – and overcomes to the point of reigning in life.* Not only will the Believer overcome sinful ways through grace, but *the Believer who receives grace will work harder for the Kingdom* than the Believer who strives in his or her own strength. Witness the declaration of the Apostle Paul, a worker of renown for the Kingdom of God, when he writes, in 1 Corinthians 15:10, 'But by the grace of God I am what I am, and His grace to me was not without effect. No, I worked harder than all of them – yet not I, but the grace of God that was with me.' Here is Paul's testimony that receiving grace produces much hard work for the Kingdom. The Christian, therefore, who is feeling unproductive for the Kingdom should not resort to striving, or assuming that God cannot use him or her; that Christian should receive grace and then serve in God's power. For those who are sufficiently caught up in their sin that they despair of ever being free of sinful ways, habits or thoughts, *the Scriptures again point to grace as the way of overcoming.* The promise to the Believer, in Romans 6:14, is that, 'Sin shall not be your master, because you are not under law, but under grace.'

Finally, Colossians 1:6 points out the absolute necessity of understanding grace in order to bear fruit and grow; it says, 'All over the world this gospel is bearing fruit and growing, just as it has been doing among you *since* the day you heard it and understood God's grace in all its truth,' (author's emphasis). *It is the understanding of grace that produces growth and fruit.*

For the reasons listed here, and others as revealed in Scripture, it is of enormous importance that Christians have a correct understanding of grace.

Some effects of not living under grace

In John 1:16 it says that, 'From the fullness of His grace we have all received one blessing after another.' In the old Covenant blessings were dependent upon obedience; in the New Covenant the blessings are freely given through grace. *The Believer who does not understand, and live under, grace risks missing out on some of God's blessings* - generally through a sense of unworthiness and a wrong belief that God will not bless Christians who are not fully 'living the life.' The problem is made worse by the fact that, in missing out on some of those blessings, the Believer may miss out on the very help needed at the particular moment of weakness that has brought about the sense of unworthiness or failure.

There are only two major Covenants between God and man - that of Moses and that of Jesus; there are other Covenants but these are the two major ones around which the Old and New Testaments of the Bible respectively revolve. The only alternative to living under grace is to live under Law, to live in a legalistic relationship with God which is based upon obedience not grace, works and not faith. The problem for the Believer in such a situation is that the Bible states that, '. . . the power of sin is the law', 1 Cor. 15:56. Those who are, for whatever reason, not living under grace are living under Law. Those who live under Law are living under the regime which gives the sin in the Believer's life its very power. *Not living under grace condemns the Believer to a life of fruitless struggle against sin* - this should be compared with the wonderful promise of Romans 6:14. *Another result of not living under grace is that it keeps the Believer immature.*

Hebrews 5:13 says, 'Anyone who lives on milk, being still an infant, is not acquainted with the teaching about righteousness.' The righteousness of the Christian is God-given. It is an act of grace by which, through the death of Jesus, the Believer is given right standing before God for all eternity. Not understanding, and living in, this truth about grace will keep the Believer immature – that is the Word of God. 2 Peter 1:9 reinforces this very point when it says that anyone who does not possess Christian qualities, listed in 2 Peter 1:5-7, in their life in increasing measure is ineffective and unproductive. Peter goes on to write that the reason for that state of affairs is that the Believer has forgotten that his or her sins have been forgiven.

Some truths about grace

Grace is independent. It can be thought of as being linked to, for example, a Believer's lifestyle or a Believer's spiritual life; however, grace is unrelated to any other matter. It is not uncommon to find Christians who believe that God is withholding His grace from them because of sin in their lives. This supposed withholding of grace may take many forms. Some may believe that, since they are not sensing His presence, God has distanced Himself from the sinning Believer. Some may believe that a current hard experience or series of hard times is evidence of withdrawn grace, and may engage upon a frantic round of soul-searching, confession, repentance and various other religious exercises. Some will see the much vaunted 'wilderness experience' or the spiritual 'valley' as evidence of God withholding His grace for a period. Such an outlook or belief ignores the most basic truth of the Christian Gospel – that ALL sin was taken away and placed upon Christ at Calvary's cross. This will be covered in other chapters in this book; suffice to say here, that the Bible clearly teaches that sin is not an issue between God and man. The reason for this is that God has already meted out His punishment for all the sins of all mankind (1 John 2:2). The issue between God and man now is belief or lack of belief in His Son Jesus Christ (John 3:18). The Believer who accepts that grace may be withheld because of sin in their life also overlooks the Scripture's teaching, expressed in John

1:16, that, 'From the fullness of His grace we have all received one blessing after another.' The blessings, including the blessing of eternal life, come to a Believer because of grace. The Believer makes no contribution towards God's decision to bless him or her. As the Believer makes no contribution towards God's decision then that must include the Believer's lifestyle at the time God decides to bless. This is borne out in Romans 5:8 which says, 'God demonstrates His own love for us in this: While we were still sinners Christ died for us.' God is gracious towards a Believer regardless of how that Believer is living and the gift of Christ, given 'while we were still sinners' and sinning, is the ultimate proof. Grace is not withheld because of sin. The parable of The Prodigal Son, in Luke 15, illustrates this truth particularly well. This truth is Good News for the Believer who is still struggling to be free of sin's entanglement and may be fearing that God will withhold His grace.

Grace is not reduced because of the way a Believer is living. Jesus Christ, the Bible says, came 'FULL of grace and truth' (John 1:14). John 1:16, as has just been quoted, says that it was 'From the FULLNESS of His grace . . .' (author's emphasis). God is not able to be partially gracious. He is not able to be less gracious or more gracious depending upon circumstances. It is in the very character of God to be gracious and He will, and indeed must, always be true to Himself. Just as grace is not withheld because of sin, so the extending of grace is not reduced because of sin. Were this to be the case then it would mean that grace was, in fact, something which had to be earned - which, in turn, would mean that it was not grace at all. (See: Eph. 2:8-9; Jas. 1:5). This truth, like the first, is Good News for the struggling Believer; that no matter what is going on in the life of a Believer, the fullness of God's grace is consistently available.

Grace carries NO strings. The very essence of grace is that it must be free and unconditional. The moment that it carries any obligation or condition then it ceases to be grace and becomes merely an exchange - God's blessings in exchange for whatever the condition is; improved lifestyle is a common supposed condition. Ephesians 1:6 testifies to the truth of the nature of grace when it says, '... to the praise of His glorious grace, which *He has freely given us* in the One He loves' (author's emphasis). The stark truth is, that despite the enormity of God's gift to man in the form of His Son Jesus, man is under no obligation whatsoever to God as a result of that gift. If the gift carries any such obligation then it is no longer a gift. This is a very important truth because it has the power to relieve struggling Christians from any sense of failing God. If the Believer is not under any obligation then he or she cannot fail God, or let God down. Grace, to be grace, is given by God without any thought of conditions or obligations. All that God, though Jesus Christ, has achieved for man is described as a gift - eternal life (John 10:28, Rom. 6:23), the Holy Spirit (Acts 1:4, Acts 2:38), repentance and forgiveness of sins (Acts 5:31), righteousness (Rom. 5:17) and so on. As a gift, God's grace - as with any gift - comes without any thought of the Giver being paid back. A gift is paid for by the Giver, not the one who receives. This truth is Good News for the Believer because it removes any need for striving in order to pay God back, or in some way to be more worthy of His grace, or to show gratitude for grace extended. It is free and unconditional - and carries no burden.

It is God's choice to be gracious, and that choice is unconnected to any other matter. Grace is extended to man as a result of a sovereign choice made by God before even man existed. 'This grace was given to us in Christ Jesus before the beginning of time' (2 Timothy 1:9). Grace is from God to man and unaffected by any contribution by man. Ephesians 2:8-9 specifically rules out any contribution by man, 'For it is by grace you have been saved, through faith - and this is not of yourselves, it is a gift of God - not by works, so that no-one can boast.'

If anything the Believer does encourages God to be gracious to the Believer then that grace is not freely given and, therefore, ceases to be grace. God treats the Believer in such a gracious way as a matter of His choice and without regard to anything done, or not done, by the Believer. The Scriptures make it quite clear that the giving of grace is entirely a matter of God's sovereign choice. Grace is not earned by the Believer nor is it in any way related to sin in the life of a Believer. In short, it is entirely unconnected to any matter except the sovereign will of God. Taking into account the nature of God, this truth is Good News for the Believer.

Grace is an expression of God's kindness. God shows mankind His kindness through His Son Jesus Christ. Ephesians 2:7 says, '...He might show the incomparable riches of His grace, expressed in His kindness to us in Christ Jesus.' Various Scriptures speak of God's kindness. Romans 2:4 tells how it is God's kindness that leads people to repentance. Romans 11:22 urges Believers to consider the kindness of God. Titus 3:4-5 speaks of how it was the appearing of God's kindness that saved Believers. In all these references to kindness, in keeping with Ephesians 2:7, the word grace can be used instead of kindness – they are one and the same thing.

God's forgiveness of the sins of a Believer is an outworking of His justice not His grace. The forgiveness that God extends to the Believer is not an act of grace. The sending of the substitute Lamb of God to bear the punishment for sin was God's act of grace. The fact that God does not punish the Believer for his or her sin is an act of God's perfect justice – the penalty has already been borne by Jesus, therefore there is no outstanding punishment due to the Christian and that is why he or she is not punished. This truth is Good News for the Christian who may be living with some belief that God may yet punish them, in some way, for their sins. It is Good News for the Christian who is still living in fear of some sort of judgement. The penalty for sin is death. Jesus has been punished instead of the Believer – that is the very Good News of the Gospel.

Examples of God's grace demonstrated through Jesus

Mark 2:1-12 Healing the paralytic. In response to the faith of the paralytic and his friends, Jesus forgives him his sins and then physically heals him. Jesus makes no demands, sets no conditions – He sees a need, sees their faith and graciously responds.

Luke 15:20-24 The welcoming of the lost son. The welcome extended to the lost son began even when the son was 'still a long way off'. The father made no demands of the son, made no enquiries about how he had spent the money, was there any left, how would it be paid back and so on. The father set down no conditions such as the son needing to work to pay back the loss. The father's one intention was to offer to restore a broken relationship, and to himself bear the cost brought about through the son's actions. In this passage is a powerful illustration of God's attitude to mankind. God is willing to bear the cost of man's actions and to graciously restore the sinner to a position as a son within God's household.

Luke 19:1-10 Zaccheus. When Jesus announced to Zaccheus, 'I must stay at your house today' He put no conditions upon His gracious offer to stay under the roof of a tax collector. He did not demand that Zaccheus stop being a tax collector. He did not demand that Zaccheus pay back anyone he had cheated. The fact is that as Zaccheus received Jesus' grace he became a changed man and voluntarily repaid those he had cheated. This is Good News for the Believer who thinks he or she will never change – the message here is that it is the receiving of grace which brings about change, not striving to be better.

John 21:15-19 Jesus reinstates Peter. After Peter denied Jesus, at the time surrounding His trial, Peter 'went outside and wept bitterly' (Luke 22:62). Jesus had already declared that whoever denied Him before men would be denied by Jesus before the Father in heaven (Matt. 10:33). With this background, and Peter's demonstrated awareness of how he had betrayed Jesus, their meeting on the beach, in this passage in John, could have been entirely different. Instead, it gives a wonderful illustration of how Jesus graciously restored His zealous, but very human, follower. What Good News for every Believer whose heart cries 'Yes, Jesus,' but whose flesh leads them down a contrary path. This encounter once again shows Jesus making no demands of Peter, no promises extracted regarding any further denials, no reprimand issued – just a gracious, freely offered reinstatement.

Romans 8:34 Christ's ongoing grace towards the Believer. This Scripture is a source of joy to the Believer who receives it. God's gracious provision did not end with Jesus' earthly mission. Now that Jesus is raised up and seated at the right hand of God, He continues His grace towards the Believer by continually, as this Scripture says, interceding for the Christian.

1 John 2:1 Christ's ongoing grace towards the Believer. This is another Scripture which confirms the security of the Believer, and the unending grace of God. Jesus Christ continuously carries out His ministry of intercession, speaking as the Scripture says, '. . . to the Father in our defence.' The Christian is both saved by grace and kept by grace.

Conclusion

The completeness of God's provision of grace, through His gift to man of His Son, Jesus, is attested to in Colossians 1:21-22, which says, 'Once you were alienated from God and were enemies in your minds because of your evil behaviour. But now He has reconciled you by Christ's physical body through death to present you ***holy in His sight, without blemish and free from accusation . . .*** ' (author's emphasis).

The Believer stands firm and reigns in life because of this grace. The need to understand this grace in order to be more effective for the Gospel is shown in Colossians 1:6, which says, 'All over the world this gospel is bearing fruit and growing, just as it has been doing among you *since* the day you heard it and understood God's grace in all its truth,' (author's emphasis).

The Believer must be rightly taught the completeness of God's gracious provision so that the Believer may, in turn, accurately pass on the *Good* News of Jesus Christ.

CHAPTER 2

Secure in grace

Introduction
There is a lot of confusion today over what a person must do in order to be saved. Such a person may be told, 'You must repent,' or 'You must ask for forgiveness,' or 'You must ask Jesus into your life/heart,' and so on. Whatever particular answer is given to the enquirer, it usually ends up with some, even a lot, of the responsibility for salvation falling upon the person. This is contrary to the truth proclaimed in Scripture which declares, 'For it is by grace you have been saved, through faith – and this not from yourselves, it is the gift of God – not by works, so that no-one can boast' Eph. 2:8-9.

The confusion which exists over how a person is saved is as nothing, though, when compared with the confusion about what a Christian contributes to his or her keeping – or losing – of salvation. It is in this area of safe-keeping that the full weight of misapplied Scripture is usually brought to bear – and most commonly upon people who are already struggling to hold onto a positive idea of how God sees them. Scriptures such as Gal. 5:19-21, 'The acts of the sinful nature are obvious; sexual immorality, impurity and debauchery; idolatry and witchcraft, fits of rage, selfish ambition, dissensions, factions and envy; drunkenness, orgies and the like. I warn you, as I did before, that those who live like this will not inherit the kingdom of God.' Such a Scripture can often be used – perhaps with the best of intent – to warn, even frighten, a Christian into some kind of self-imposed improvement in lifestyle. Another Scripture which is often used in the same role is Heb. 10:26-27. 'If we deliberately keep on sinning after we have received the knowledge of the truth, no sacrifice for sins is left, but only a fearful expectation of judgement and of raging fire that will consume the enemies of God.'

In the light of such Scriptures many a Christian has been robbed of the joy of their salvation. The lightness of spirit, the love of God, the close walk which was experienced at salvation is gradually replaced by striving. The lightness is replaced by a heaviness of spirit, the joy is replaced by uncertainty and fear and the close walk becomes a distant relationship which seems to grow colder, and more difficult to maintain, with each passing sermon.

All this occurs in the name of safeguarding one's salvation; yet the Scriptures make it plain that not only are Christians saved by grace, but Christians are also kept safe, for now and for all eternity, by that same grace. Rom. 5:1-2 says, 'Therefore, since we have been justified through faith, we have peace with God through our Lord Jesus Christ, through whom we have gained access by faith into this grace in which we now stand.' Saved by grace, standing by grace – one of many such Scriptures.

The purpose of this chapter is to look at the issues which establish that just as a Christian's salvation is entirely a work of God for man, so that Christian's safe-keeping is, also, entirely a work of God for man. The issues to be looked at are (I) The fundamental truth of grace, (II) God's purposes for the Christian and (III) God's provision for the Christian.

(I) The fundamental truth of grace

There are many basic truths about grace, some of which have already been examined in an earlier chapter, but there is one fundamental truth about grace which underpins all other truths about grace. *The one fundamental truth about grace is that grace is freely and undeservedly given.* It is from this truth that all other truths about grace will flow. It is this one fundamental truth which assures the Christian of his or her security in salvation. As grace is freely and undeservedly given, then it is given without regard to what is going on in the life of the recipient, either at the time grace is extended or thereafter. This means that **grace is given** to the recipient:

(i) Without regard to sin.
A person becomes a Believer by accepting that he or she is a lost sinner and by trusting in Jesus Christ for their salvation. That trust is based on the truth that when Jesus died on Calvary's cross, He was being punished for every sin the Believer had committed or ever would commit. Thus, God maintains His perfect justice, and His hatred of sin, and yet is able to be gracious towards the sinner. This situation is maintained after the point of conversion. In other words, although the Christian probably will go on sinning, God will continue to extend His grace and blessings to that person – including the gracious blessing (and free gift) of eternal life – because the sacrifice of Jesus has already paid for the sins committed before *and after* conversion. There is only one answer to sin and that is the blood of Christ shed on the cross. That answer applies to all sins for all people for all time. In the Bible it says, in 1 John 2:2, 'He [Jesus] is the atoning sacrifice for our sins, and not only for ours but also for the sins of the whole world.' This Scripture, and many others, make it clear that sin is no longer an issue between God and man. The issue now, the Scriptures make clear, is belief in or rejection of Jesus as the Son of God. John 3:18 says that a person stands condemned, '. . . because he has not believed in the name of God's one and only Son.' The issue between God and man is not the details of how a person lives their individual, daily life; but what that person believes about Jesus. That is why, without compromising His divine justice, God can still regard a sinning Christian as His saved child. A Christian is saved, and remains saved, because of faith in Christ's achievement on his or her behalf, not by works. Thus the fundamental truth about grace – that it is freely and undeservedly given – ensures that the subsequent lifestyle of the Christian has no effect at all on their standing before God, either in this life or in the one to come. Any teaching that instils insecurity and fear into a Christian about their standing before God is rooted in a works-centred salvation and, as such, stands opposed to the cross of Christ and should be resolutely resisted.

(ii) Without regard to the response.

Grace, to be grace, has to be freely given. This means that it is extended by God to man without any strings or conditions. The Scriptures always refer to eternal life as a gift and, in order to be a gift, it has to be free. The truth has to be that if the gift of eternal life is to remain a gift then it has to be given without regard to the response of the recipient. The reality has to be that God's gift of His Son Jesus, and all that flows through Him, puts the Christian under no obligation whatsoever. This lack of obligation must include the lack of obligation to live in a certain way or according to a certain standard. It is the lifestyle of a Christian subsequent to salvation that is so often used as the source of threat to their eternal security and salvation. Yet the truth is that the lifestyle prior to or subsequent to conversion has no bearing at all on the Christian's standing before God and, therefore, their security in salvation. If a Christian accepts any obligation as a result of the gift of salvation – the commonest being that the Christian should strive against sin and seek to improve his or her way of life – then that Christian puts God, effectively, in the supposed position of saying, 'I give you eternal life as a free gift; but in order to keep that gift you are required to . . .' Such is the substance of so much teaching today. Christians are continually told that God's attitude towards them, even to including their eternal salvation, fluctuates according to the Christian's daily lifestyle and effort. Such teaching flies in the face of a mass of Scripture. Those who teach such error do so because they have not understood the empowerment that comes through grace and wrongly see grace, fully embraced, as a road to licence. This is dealt with in a subsequent chapter. Thus the fundamental truth about grace – that it is freely and undeservedly given – ensures that the response of the Christian, subsequent to salvation, has no relevance at all to their standing before God, either in this life or in the one to come. Any teaching to the contrary tarnishes the great gift of Jesus, reduces that gift to a mere exchange and should be, again, resolutely resisted.

(II) God's purposes for the Christian

There are in the Scriptures two identifiable purposes behind God's grace towards the Christian and both these purposes ensure the Christian's safe-keeping in grace, removing from the Christian the often held fear of slipping from grace and the losing of their salvation. The two purposes are:

(i) The *future* displaying of God's grace
Ephesians 2:6-7 says, 'And God raised us up with Christ and seated us with Him in the heavenly realms in Christ Jesus *in order that* **in the coming ages** He might show the incomparable riches of His grace, expressed in His kindness to us in Christ Jesus' (author's emphasis). This Scripture shows that the purpose behind God's grace towards the Christian will not be fulfilled until 'the coming ages.' There are two things to consider about this Scripture with regard to a Christian's security in salvation. Firstly, if a Christian contributes anything at all towards his being 'raised up and seated with Christ' then God will not be able to display that Christian as a trophy of pure grace. Yet it is God's intention, in a time still to come, to show through the Believer in heaven the breadth and depth of God's amazing grace. It can be safely said, therefore, that a Christian will contribute nothing at all to his being in heaven – and equally, therefore, the Christian cannot risk his place in heaven, nor his standing before God, by anything he does or does not do. The Christian remains secure in his salvation because of grace and God's purpose in that grace. The second thing to say about this Scripture is that God's purpose in grace is not fulfilled when the Christian becomes saved. God's purpose will not be fulfilled until 'the coming ages.' If a Christian's safe-keeping in salvation depended, in any way, upon the Christian's contribution then God could have no guarantee that He would be left with any trophies of grace to display. For the Christian to be the witness 'in the coming ages' to God's grace then the Christian must be saved by grace and must be kept secure in salvation by that same grace. God's purpose will be fulfilled only because God is the guarantor.

(ii) The outworking of *pre-determined* good works
In Ephesians 2:10 it says, 'For we are God's workmanship, *created in Christ Jesus to do good works which God prepared in*

advance for us to do,' (author's emphasis). If the Christian's standing in the faith, or the continuance of his right relationship with God, depends in any way upon the Christian's contribution or effort then God could have no confidence that the works He prepared in advance for the Christian to do would be completed. If any of these works, predetermined by God, was not completed then that would entirely discredit the Bible which states, in Job 42:2, when speaking of God that, '... no plan of Yours can be thwarted.' God Himself says, in Isaiah 14:24, that, 'Surely, as I have planned, so it will be, and as I have purposed, so it will stand.' God could safely prepare good works in advance for the Christian only because He knows that it is He who will both save the Christian and, thereafter, keep the Christian saved and that, therefore, the Christian will be enabled to complete those predetermined tasks.

God can only have long-term purposes in grace, as the two outlined here, if He, and He alone, is the guarantor that those purposes will be fulfilled. The promise of 1 Corinthians 1:8 says just that; 'He [God] will keep you strong to the end...'

(III) God's provision for the Christian

The Scriptures show the many provisions which God has made for the Christian in order that, having been saved, he may remain safe and secure in his salvation through his keeping *in* grace, and *by* grace. The many provisions which God has made for the Believer all involve the very Person of God in the different roles of the Holy Trinity – Father, Son and Holy Spirit. God is wholly engaged in saving and keeping safe the Christian.

(i) God the Father – His power

In John 10:29 the Lord Jesus says, 'My Father who has given them [the Believers] to Me is greater than all; no-one can snatch them out of My Father's hand.' The Believer is nestled in the hand of God the Father. The power of God guarantees the Christian's security. No-one, no power, can snatch the Believer from the position he occupies in the Father's hand. Paul expresses his confidence in the keeping power of God when, in 2 Timothy 1:12, he writes, '... I know whom I have believed, and am convinced that He is able to guard what I have entrusted to Him for that day.' Paul's faith, his confidence, is in God's ability to maintain Paul's position - not in Paul's ability to maintain his own position. Satan is a created being, perhaps more powerful than human beings, but not more powerful - or even as powerful - as the God who created all things. Satan cannot snatch the Christian out of God's hand, and with God guarding the Christian, Satan cannot entice or lure the Christian away - for God will not allow that. The Christian is kept perfectly safe by the power of God Himself. Jude acknowledges this in verse 24 of his letter. He writes, 'To Him who is able to keep you from falling and to present you before His glorious presence without fault and with great joy...' It is God who keeps the Christian from falling. Such understanding from the Bible of God's role in the Christian's security brings great peace and joy, and, in keeping with the rest of the Gospel, is Good News.

(ii) God the Father – His love

Romans 8:39 says, '... nor anything else in all creation will be able to separate us [the Believers] from the love of God that is in Christ Jesus.' There is no power in the universe that can separate the Believer from the love which God has for him or her. When it is written that nothing can separate the Christian from the love of God then that must include the very things that Christians fear will bring about that separation - and the biggest of these is usually the lifestyle of the Christian after salvation. God's love, though, is able to absorb even that. It should be remembered by the Christian who fears that God may stop showing him or her His love that '... God demonstrates His own love for us in this: While we were still sinners, Christ died for us' Romans 5:8. It was while the Christian was still caught up in his sin that God sent His Son - such is the power of His love; a love that saves, a love that secures.

(iii) Christ – His prayer

In John 17, at the last supper, Jesus prayed. He prayed for His disciples and then, in verse 20, He prayed, 'My prayer is not for them [the disciples] alone. I pray also for those who will believe in

Me through their message.' Jesus declared the content of His prayer in verse 15, 'My prayer is not that You [the Father] take them out of the world but that You protect them from the evil one'. How can a Christian live in fear that in some way Satan will snatch him away or entice him away from God? Jesus Christ has asked the Father to protect the Christian from those very things - '. . . protect them from the evil one.' Of course the Christian will have trouble in this world, Jesus Himself said so. Those troubles, though, will never empower Satan to entice or snatch away the Christian. God the Son asked God the Father to protect the Christian from the evil one. Every Christian should be very, very secure that having been saved, he or she will remain safe in their salvation - because God the Father will very obviously grant the prayer of God the Son.

(iv) Christ – His blood
The Bible says, '. . . without the shedding of blood there is no forgiveness' (Hebrews 9:22). There are many Scriptures in the New Testament that tell of what Christ has achieved for man through the shedding of His blood. Hebrews 13:12 says that, '. . . Jesus also suffered outside the city gate to make the people holy through His own blood.' It is the blood of Jesus that secures holiness for the Believer and not, as is so often taught, the Believer's own striving. The blood has been shed and the holiness secured. Let every Christian rest in Christ's achievement.

(v) Christ – His death
When Jesus Christ died the Bible says - in Rom. 8:3 - that through His death God 'condemned sin in sinful man.' As Paul wrote in regard to sin, in Rom. 7:17, '. . . it is no longer I myself who do it but it is sin living in me.' Sin is condemned, not the Christian. The death of Jesus achieved that for the Christian. John 3:18 makes it clear that rejection of Jesus is the only reason left for condemnation. A Believer has accepted Jesus Christ. Jesus' death pays the penalty for every sin ever committed by anyone (1 John 2:2). A fundamental provision of God for the salvation, and the subsequent security of the Christian, is the death of Jesus. It is His

death that gives the truth to the Scripture, Rom. 8:1, 'Therefore, there is now no condemnation for those who are in Christ Jesus.'

(vi) Christ – His resurrection
Romans 6:3-4 explains that the Christian has, through faith, shared with Christ in His death and burial. Romans 6:5 goes on to say, 'If we have been united with Him like this in His death, we will certainly also be united with Him in His resurrection.' The resurrected life of Jesus Christ is within every Believer - that guarantees the safety of the Believer, for who can stand against Christ?

(vii) Christ – His intercession
In 1 John 2:1 it says, 'My dear children, I write this to you so that you will not sin. But if anybody does sin, we have One who speaks to the Father in our defence - Jesus Christ, the Righteous One.' It is not the job of the Christian to plead his cause before the Father - there is One in heaven, Jesus Christ, who does that for the Believer. Christ has to be the One who speaks for the Christian, for what could the Christian say on his own behalf? Could he ask for clemency? Could he promise never to sin again? Even if he could make such a promise it would achieve nothing - God demands a death penalty for every sin (Rom. 6:23). Jesus Christ, as the One who died for sinners, is the only One qualified to speak for sinners. Hebrews 9:12 says that Christ entered the Most Holy Place by means of His own blood. It is through His shed blood that Jesus is able to be an effective advocate for the sinning Believer, and so keep that Believer safe.

(viii) Christ – His shepherdhood
In John 10:11 Jesus says, 'I am the good shepherd'. The good shepherd does not wait until his flock is attacked and then seek to defend his sheep. The good shepherd protects his flock by preventing the attack. Jesus Christ illustrates this care in Luke 22:31-32 when He informs Peter, who is unaware of the danger, 'Simon, Simon, Satan has asked to sift you as wheat. But I have prayed for you, Simon, that your faith may not fail . . .' Jesus Christ

knows what Satan is up to and Jesus is eternally guarding and protecting His people against the schemes of the enemy. The Christian need have no fear. Peter confirms this eternal shepherding ministry of Christ when he writes of Jesus, in 1 Peter 2:25, 'For you were like sheep going astray, but now you have returned to the Shepherd and Overseer of your souls.' Once again, it can be seen that the secure position of the Christian depends upon Jesus and not upon the Christian.

(ix) The Spirit – bringing new birth

In John 1:12-13 there are important truths which establish the secure, and unalterable, position of the Believer. The verses say, 'Yet to all who received Him, to those who believed in His name, He gave the right to become children of God – children born not of natural descent, nor of human decision or a husband's will, but born of God.' It is 'to those who believed' that God gave *the right* to be called His children. This entirely removes any consideration of lifestyle subsequent to that spiritual birth. All Believers are born of the Spirit (John 3:5-6). Nothing can alter the parentage of the Believer or, therefore, the Believer's position as a child within the family of God. Faith was the key to entry into the family of God – and that faith was given by God (1 Cor. 12:3, Eph. 2:8). That God-given faith gives the Believer the right to be a child of God. It is not a privilege which can be taken away at any point. A Believer is a child of God because that is his right. God Himself has secured that right by giving the Believer that faith which enabled his spiritual birth. The Believer is totally secure because of this provision by God for his security.

(x) The Spirit – ensuring new life

The Bible says that the Spirit of God lives within every Believer. In John 7:39 it explains that the 'rivers of living water' referred to by Jesus in the previous verse is '. . . the Spirit, whom those who believed in Him were later to receive.' In John 14:16 it is Jesus who says that He will ask the Father to give '. . . another Counsellor to be with you [the Believers] forever – the Spirit of truth.' Romans 5:5 speaks of God's love being poured out into the Believer's heart

'. . . by the Holy Spirit, whom He has given us.' There are other verses which speak of the indwelling Spirit and also explain His role in the life of a Believer. Jesus asked that the indwelling Spirit be with the Believer 'for ever' (John 14:16). If the Spirit can be quenched or grieved away from the Believer then it means that Jesus' prayer in John 14:16 has gone unanswered - a ridiculous concept. The Spirit safeguards the Believer for, again, who can stand against God?

(xi) The Spirit – 'sealing' the Believer
Every Believer is said, in the Bible, to be sealed with the Holy Spirit. In 2 Corinthians 1:22 it speaks of the fact that God has put His seal of ownership on the Believer and 'put His Spirit in our hearts as a deposit, guaranteeing what is to come.' It is the Holy Spirit of God who is the guarantor of the Christian's eternal inheritance. There can be no room for fear or doubt in the heart of a Christian when such Scriptures are understood. Ephesians 1:13-14 says very much the same thing and Ephesians 4:30 speaks again of the Believer having been sealed with the Spirit, and in this verse, it gives the time span of that sealing - it is 'until the day of redemption.' Although a Believer may grieve the Spirit or quench the Spirit, nevertheless the Spirit remains with the Believer 'until the day of redemption.' The Believer can be forever secure in his or her salvation upon the basis of this sealing of the Believer by the Spirit.

(xii) The Believer's position in Christ
The Believer is united with Christ, by the Spirit, to the extent that he is said to be 'in Christ.' This identification with Christ, because the Christian is 'in Christ,' brings with it the truth that the Believer is now, and forever will be, accepted by God - who sees the Believer as 'clothed . . . with Christ' (Gal. 3:27). The Believer's position 'in Christ' is a work of God for man. In 1 Corinthians 1:30 it says, 'It is because of Him [God] that you are in Christ Jesus . . .' Having placed the Believer 'in Christ' it says in 2 Corinthians 1:21, 'Now it is God who makes both us and you stand firm in Christ.' It can be seen, then, that it is God who places the Believer in Christ,

it is God who causes the Believer to remain (stand firm) in Christ and it is God who accepts the Believer because of his position 'in Christ.' Saved by grace and kept by that same grace.

Summary
The truth of safe-keeping through grace is revealed through:
I. *The fundamental truth of grace*, which means grace is extended:
   (i) without regard to sin and,
   (ii) without regard to the response.
II. *The purposes of God in grace*, which are not fulfilled at initial salvation, making it necessary for God to keep the saved sinner by grace in order for His purposes to be fulfilled.
III. *The many provisions and safeguards which God has made*, including Himself, His Son and the Holy Spirit, for the purpose of keeping safe the saved sinner.

Salvation by grace is the purpose of God's redemption through Christ. Failure to trust in Christ alone is seen when salvation is supposed to depend on anything other than believing in Christ, and when a Christian's security in salvation is made to depend at any point on his or her own effort or contribution. The Believer contributes nothing to being saved and nothing to being kept saved. It is all a work of God for man – and that's Good News.

CHAPTER 3

Grace: easy option or source of power?

Introduction

The great debate about grace in the Christian church is about whether by embracing grace fully a Christian will inevitably lapse into licence or abuse of grace. A study of the Bible reveals that grace is always taught as being the source of power within a Christian's life. It is a common misteaching today that unless checks and balances are put in place the Christian risks ending up in the position, described in Jude 1:4, of changing '. . . the grace of our God into a licence for immorality. . .'

The issue upon which the church needs to rethink its teaching is not 'How should a Christian live' – for that issue is not under debate. The Bible makes it quite clear that Christians are commanded into holy living. The issue is, 'How does the Christian achieve that holy living?' The Bible teaches that it is by receiving grace, yet generally the church teaches that it is a mixture of receiving grace and striving. Such wrong teaching is responsible for much misery within many committed Christians who feel they are failing to make the grade. Every individual Christian, and the church as a whole, needs to understand that grace is a 'power word' and is the source of obedience and holy living – not the road to licence.

Two inseparable truths

There are two inseparable truths revealed in the grace teachings within the New Covenant. The misteaching that goes on today occurs because these truths have been separated. The first truth is the standard of living which God requires from the Christian who is already saved by, and living under, grace. The second truth is that the life under grace is to be lived in sole, and total, dependence on the enabling power of the Holy Spirit. If these truths are, as is so common today, separated then the Christian is left, if the first truth is taught separately, with an impossibly high standard of living to which he has been left to struggle to reach in his own strength. This is the position in which untold numbers of Christians find themselves, and it is a position which creates the cycle of striving, failing, recommitting, striving, failing and so on. If, on the other hand, the second truth is taught without regard to the first, then the Christian is left with an indulgent, self-centred life which lacks any spiritual direction or discipline.

God's standard for the Christian

A look through the Scriptures which detail how God wants His children to live quickly shows the foolishness of even trying to live up to such a standard in human strength. In Matthew 5 Jesus teaches that, whereas under the Old Covenant the requirement was simply not to murder another person, now God requires that His children do not even get angry at another. In Matthew 19:21 Jesus says that anyone wishing to be perfect should sell their possessions, give to the poor and then follow Him. In 1 Corinthians 1:2 it is made clear to Believers that we are 'called to be holy.' Ephesians 4:29 commands the Believers to '. . . not let any unwholesome talk come out of your mouths.' Christians are instructed, in Philippians 2:5, that their attitude should be the same as that of Jesus. And so it goes on. Calls to holiness, commands to live as a 'living sacrifice', commands to be sanctified. It is very easy to see how, if taken on their own, God's commands and directions to His children represent an enormous challenge, which rapidly becomes an enormous burden.

The Holy Spirit meets God's standard

Many Christians lose the joy of their salvation, missing out on being a vital witness, because they spend so much time striving to effect change in their lives. In Luke 24:49 Jesus promised His disciples that He would send what His Father had promised and that they would be 'clothed with power from on high.' The promise was fulfilled with the gift, and the power, being received at Pentecost (Acts 2). Jesus also instructed His followers that the changes in their lives would come from within them – and not be the external result of self-imposed discipline. These teachings come in John 7:38-39, where Jesus tells His followers that 'streams of living waters will flow from within' them and the Bible then goes on to explain that, 'By this He meant the Spirit . . .' It is the life of the Spirit of God, flowing in the life of a Christian, that brings change in the Christian and change in the world. It is not an improved way of life which the Christian has managed to achieve; it is a new life, God's life, that brings glory to Jesus. In Acts 1:8 Jesus tells His followers that they will receive power 'when the Spirit comes on you.' Romans 8:11 tells of how it is the Spirit who 'will also give life to your mortal bodies.'

Philippians 2:13 again addresses the issue of the power in a Christian's life when it reassures Believers that it is 'God who works in you to will and to act according to His good purpose.' These Scriptures, and a host of others, all fit in entirely with the Gospel of Grace as revealed by Jesus Christ. All of them put the responsibility for Christian living fairly and squarely onto God. Those who think this is merely the Christian opting out of his or her responsibility need only look back to the revealed standard that God requires from the Christian. It is a standard that only God Himself can achieve. It is not an opt out for the Christian to hand over responsibility for his daily living to God; it is the only hope that Christian has of living in the way the God desires and commands.

The Spirit of Grace

In both the Old and the New Testaments the Holy Spirit is referred to as 'the Spirit of grace' – Zechariah 12:10, Heb. 10:29. In the context of salvation, Jesus is God's gift of grace to man – freely and undeservedly given. In the context of daily living, the Holy Spirit is God's gift to man. **Grace as a source of power can be clearly understood when that grace is seen as the Holy Spirit, the Spirit of grace, within the Christian.** Correctly understood in this way, it makes no sense whatsoever to put any restraint upon receiving, and living in, grace; for this truly means to receive and live in the power of the Holy Spirit. As long as the full Gospel message is taught – which includes the high standard to which the Christian is called – then any tendency towards indulgence is curbed and the power-filled life has direction and meaning. Grace, seen in the context of being the Holy Spirit, can never be an easy option, it can only ever be the source of obedience within the Christian's life. This is what Jesus taught and this is what the Bible teaches throughout the New Testament.

Christ's dependence upon the Holy Spirit

The Bible makes it clear that Jesus lived in dependence upon the Holy Spirit. In this, as in all things, He is the example and role model Christians follow. Jesus specifically stated, in John 5:19, that '... the Son can do nothing by Himself.' And that is the state within which every Christian can rest, accepting their own limitations and allowing God to 'will and to act according to His good purpose (Phil. 2:13). The starting point for Jesus, and therefore the Christian, was to be able to do nothing in His own strength. The Bible then reveals how Jesus lived in total dependence upon the Spirit of God throughout His earthly life.

In Luke 1:35 the birth of Jesus is attributed to an act by the Holy Spirit and in Romans 1:4 it is the Spirit who is credited with identifying Jesus as the Son of God, as a result of Christ's resurrection from the dead. So from the beginning of His earthly life, until beyond His resurrection, Jesus is dependent upon the Holy Spirit. At the beginning of His ministry, when Jesus was baptized, the Holy Spirit descended upon Jesus – thus identifying Him as the Son of God (John 1:34). Following His baptism Jesus was led by the Spirit into the desert (Matt. 4:1) and, after a forty day fast, returned 'in the power of the Spirit' (Luke 4:14). In His public declaration of His ministry Jesus acknowledges that it is the Spirit who is directing His life by declaring, 'The Spirit of the Lord is on Me ...' (Luke 4:18). Later in His ministry Jesus is described as being, '... full of joy through the Holy Spirit ...' (Luke 10:21). Jesus also acknowledged His dependence upon the Father in John 5:19, as has already been quoted; in John 5:30, when He declares, 'By Myself I can do nothing', as well as in John 8:28 and again in John 14:10. The need for divine empowerment in Jesus' life is shown during His agony in Gethsemane when, in Luke 22:43, an angel was sent to strengthen Him. Jesus demonstrates His willingness to depend upon His Father when, as He is about to be arrested and Peter seeks to prevent the arrest, He tells Peter, in Matt. 26:52-53, 'Put your sword back in its place . . . Do you think I cannot call upon My Father, and He will at once put at My disposal more than twelve legions of angels?'

Jesus' birth, His ministry, His life, His death, His resurrection and His being recognized as the Son of God were all under the control and direction of the Holy Spirit – the Spirit of grace.

The way we think

The Bible teaches a great deal about the importance of the way a Christian thinks and how that thinking affects how the Christian lives. One very clear area where the Christian needs to get his thinking in line with Scriptural revelation is in the area of empowerment – and the role of grace in that empowerment. In Romans 12:2 the Bible says that it is possible to completely change the way we live, simply by getting a new way of thinking – '. . . be transformed by the renewing of your mind.' This is contrary to human wisdom. Human beings find it hard to grasp the idea that lives can change without a great deal of effort. That is why Christians are repeatedly pointed to their own efforts when it comes to dealing with issues in their lives. The Church, and the individual Christian, must heed the words of the Apostle Paul, in Ephesians 4:17, when he says, 'So I tell you this, and insist on it in the Lord, that you must no longer live as the Gentiles do, in the futility of their thinking.' It is significant that Paul, when referring to the Gentiles, is not attacking their lifestyle, but the 'futility of their thinking.' Likewise for the Christian today, it is not lifestyle that needs to be focused upon and changed; it is the Christian's way of thinking.

Current thinking can include the idea that Christians have to strive against sin, that Christians have to, in some way, please God with their lifestyle, that Christians have to get rid of something in their lives, or start something in their lives, in order to be more acceptable to God. Anyone labouring under such ideas needs, as

Paul goes on to write in Ephesians 4:23, to '... be made new in the attitude of your minds.'

Thinking, grace and empowerment

Jesus said that when the Spirit came He would lead us into a knowledge of all truth (John 16:13). Jesus had already told His followers, in John 8:32, that 'the truth will set you free.' From these two Scriptures it can be seen that it is the Spirit of grace who will set the Christian free. In John 17:17, Jesus, whilst praying, says that it is the truth that sanctifies the Believer. Again, tying this in with John 16:13, it can be seen that the Scriptures reveal it is the responsibility of the Spirit to sanctify the Believer. This freedom and sanctification come as the Believer receives the truth as revealed by the Holy Spirit - the Spirit of grace. The fundamental truth of the Gospel is expressed in 2 Corinthians 5:18-19. Paul has been writing about the fact that the Christian is a new creation in Christ. He goes on to say, 'All this is from God, who reconciled us to Himself through Christ and gave us the ministry of reconciliation: that God was reconciling the world to Himself in Christ, not counting men's sins against them.' In receiving that one truth - that God does not count men's sins against them - there is enormous release and freedom for the Believer who simply, for whatever reason, has not managed to put sinful ways behind them - which in reality is every Christian, with only the degree of obvious sinfulness being different. How the Believer thinks on the issue of sin in their relationship with God will dramatically affect their whole Christian walk. The Bible encourages Christians, in Hebrews 4:16, to 'approach the throne of grace with confidence, so that we may receive mercy and find grace to help us in our time of need.' That confidence, and therefore that help, cannot come unless the Christian can receive the truth of how God sees his 'sins.' Paul says that the result of God 'not counting men's sins against them' is that the Christian is now reconciled to God - and it is God who did the reconciling. These are fantastic truths which not only set free, they make alive the Christian and restore the joy of salvation. The Holy Spirit reveals truths which build up, encourage and inspire the Believer. The Spirit will reveal truths which bring hope, joy, peace and love to the Believer. The Spirit will reveal the Good News of how God sees the Christian. The Believer should receive these truths and live in the empowerment they bring – the empowerment which only grace can bring.

Grace as a source of power can be clearly understood when that grace is seen as the receiving of the truths which the Holy Spirit, the Spirit of grace, would have the Christian receive and which will set free and sanctify the Believer.

True Christian growth

Many Christians find it hard to believe that God will find them acceptable unless they are striving against sin. Many teachers and preachers encourage the idea that Christian growth is about improving the way of life led by a Christian, the putting aside of some sinful habit or the adopting of a more obviously Christian habit such as daily Scripture reading or a more consistent prayer life. As usual, with all such erroneous teaching, the emphasis and focus is upon what the Christian is doing – rather than, in line with the Gospel, on what God is doing.

Christians need to follow the Biblical instruction, contained in 2 Peter 3:18, in order to experience true Christian growth. In this Scripture Peter writes, 'But grow in the grace and knowledge of our Lord and Saviour Jesus Christ.' God, through Peter, is not content for Christians to become complacent and to be satisfied with whatever stage of spiritual development they have reached. God wants Christians to grow and He uses Peter to inform Christians of the areas within which He wants them to grow. Christians should grow in grace and in their knowledge of Jesus Christ. Growth in these two areas will affect the way a Christian thinks, which, as has been written earlier, will then affect the way a Christian lives. God does want to bring about change in the way most Christians live; but He wants the change to come about in the right way, and not through continual striving and self-help. Changing God's way ensures that change does not become a burdensome process with only short-lived gains.

A brief look at the early church and their priorities, as revealed in Acts 2:42, shows where they directed their efforts. It says, 'They devoted themselves to the apostles' teaching and to the fellowship, to the breaking of bread and to prayer.' The effect of these four devotions can be seen by reading the book of Acts. The early church did many other activities; but these four devotions were their priority. In fact, when the practical issues - such as feeding widows - became too demanding, the apostles appointed deacons so that they, the apostles, could, '. . . give our attention to prayer and the ministry of the Word.' (Acts 6:4). Christians today need to follow the example of the early church and put their energies into activities which will renew their minds and give them a new way of thinking.

A devotion to the Word of God will reveal the life-changing truths that the sin issue is completely settled between the Christian and God, that the Believer is saved and kept by grace alone, that the Believer is loved, accepted and blessed by God because of Jesus, without regard to the Believer's lifestyle or effort and that the Believer is a child of God who, seeing the Believer permanently clothed in Christ, will never turn the Believer away and will never be displeased with the Believer. Receiving grace, by receiving these truths through the ministry of the Spirit of grace, will change the way a Believer sees himself and the way he sees God.

Following on from that comes the devotion to the fellowship. Having received self-acceptance, through the revealed truth of God's Word, the Believer is then able to accept his fellow Believer. Jesus said, 'All men will know that you are My disciples if you love one another' (John 13:35). The witness of personal faith is not an obvious striving against sin, but a love for fellow Believers. This can only come after self-acceptance has been received.

The devotion to the breaking of bread is a constant reminder of the cross, and all that Jesus achieved for the Believer at Calvary. It was never supposed to be a once a week ritual carried out in church. Believers need to regain the spiritual power and renewal that comes through frequent breaking of bread. This simple act is a powerful reminder of every aspect of the Good News - God's love, sin punished and done away with, new hope, new life, reconciliation to God, death defeated and so on.

Having developed a confidence in who the Believer is, having enjoyed the unity that comes through knowing that every Believer is totally, and always, dependent upon the grace of God, having developed the habit of frequently coming to the foot of the cross, through the breaking of bread, then the Believer is empowered to develop a prayer life that, in turn, really develops that Believer's relationship with his or her Father. Let love grow. Jesus Christ promises every Believer who fears licence, 'If you love Me, you will obey what I command' (John 14:15).

It is a sequence revealed in the Bible. It is a lifestyle that brought amazing results in the early church. It is a lifestyle that is now neglected by most of the modern church who, instead, are encouraged to strive against the flesh in a very fleshly manner. Let every Christian stop the striving, let every Christian revel in the relationship which has been purchased for them by Jesus, let every Christian receive the grace of God - the gift of His Son and the gift of His Spirit - and let every Christian give glory to God for the changes that He will bring into the lives of Believers who will only receive.

Grace-empowered living

The Bible teaches that it is through faith that Christians enter into grace, and that it is by grace that Christians stand - Romans 5:2. The following Scriptures represent a small selection of the Scriptures which illustrate that grace, far from being an easy option, is the very source of power in the life of every Christian: Acts 6:8, Romans 5:2, Romans 5:17, Romans 6:14, Romans 12:6, Romans 15:15-16, 1 Corinthians 1:4-5, 1 Corinthians 3:10, 1 Corinthians 15:10, 2 Corinthians 1:12, 2 Corinthians 4:15, 2 Corinthians 9:8, 2 Corinthians 12:9, Galatians 2:9, Ephesians 3:7-8, Colossians 1:6, 2 Thessalonians 2:16, 2 Timothy 1:9, 2 Timothy 2:1, Titus 2:11-12, Hebrews 4:16, 1 Peter 4:10.

A look through these Scriptures reveal grace as a source of power, a source of obedience, a source of thanksgiving, a source of witnessing and service. At no point do the Scriptures ever reveal grace as an alternative to obedience or as an easy option.

Examples from the life and teachings of Jesus

In Luke 7:36-50 is the story of how a sinful woman receives grace and, through that, is empowered to carry out costly acts of service. Verse 47 carries the key to understanding the story, and also understanding how grace empowers. Jesus, in verse 47, explains that, 'Therefore, I tell you, her many sins have been forgiven – for she loved much. But he who has been forgiven little loves little.' Christians do not need to spend their time striving against some sinful habit. Christians need to receive the forgiveness which God, in Christ, freely offers. This will, according to Jesus Himself – and illustrated in the passage in Luke – increase the love of the Christian and, through that, increase the power to serve.

This point is reinforced by Jesus through the parable He tells during the sequence of events in Luke 7:36-50. In verses 41-42 Jesus tells the very short parable known as the Parable of the Two Debtors. Again Jesus makes the point that whoever knows the greater forgiveness will love the more. And love, as Jesus says in John 14:15, is the source of Christian obedience.

In Luke 15:11-32 is what is known as the Parable of the Prodigal Son. A major teaching point within the parable is how the younger son comes home with the attitude of a servant and, through receiving the undeserved love of his father, is turned from a would-be servant into a son; a powerful illustration of how receiving grace has the power to totally transform a life. Receiving grace has the same effect upon Zaccheus in Luke 19. Zaccheus is changed from an outcast into a son of Abraham, generously supporting the poor.

In John 4, Jesus' acceptance and affirmation of an outcast Samaritan woman turns her into an outstanding evangelist capable of bringing her whole town to Jesus. In John 21, Jesus' reaffirmation of Peter paves the way for Peter to become the one who announces the Good News to the Jews and, later, to the Gentiles.

These teachings and examples, and many others not listed here, from the life of Jesus again show that it is grace which empowers and enables the Christian. The Church has almost completely lost this understanding and application of grace and sees it, instead, as a gift to be treated with caution for fear of falling into licence.

Such teaching only illustrates the lack of Biblical understanding on the part of the teacher. Let every Christian embrace grace with everything that is within them. May every Christian know the thrill of God's total acceptance, the joy of a full and secure salvation and the power of God's life being lived through them.

Summary

Grace is always taught in the Scriptures within the context of transforming power. God reveals through Christ the standard of life He expects from His children.

Christ spoke of, and demonstrated, His total dependence upon the Holy Spirit. God gives His children the same Spirit of grace by whom they may achieve the standard laid down.

The Bible reveals that the only obstacle to the Believer living within the achievement of Calvary is the way the Believer thinks. By renewing his mind and accepting the full truths of the Good News, revealed in the Scriptures, the Bible teaches that the Believer will be completely transformed.

As with the whole revelation of the Good News, the focus in the process of sanctification is on what God has done, is doing and will continue to do for man – and never on what man is doing, or should do, for God.

Further Scriptures

The following Scriptures further illustrate how God's grace is the source of blessing and power within the Believer's life:

Acts 20:32	The Word of grace builds up the Believer;
Rom. 8:11	It is the Spirit who gives life to the Believer's mortal body;
Rom. 15:16	Christians are required to be sanctified, it is the Spirit who sanctifies the Believer;
1 Cor. 16:13	The Believer will stand firm through faith;
2 Cor. 1:24	Again the encouragement to stand by faith;
2 Cor. 13:4	The Christian lives by God's power;
Phil. 3:9	Righteousness comes by faith in Christ;
1 John 5:4	It is faith, not willpower, that enables the Christian to overcome.

According to Hebrews 4:2, it is lack of faith, not lack of effort, that prevents the Believer entering into God's blessings. Grace opens up every blessing of heaven (John 1:16), faith allows the Believer to enter into grace (Rom. 5:2) and, through that, into the blessings.

May that be the experience of every Christian.

CHAPTER 4

Jesus' grace parables

Introduction
Speaking of Jesus Christ, the Apostle John writes in his Gospel, chapter 1 verse 14, 'The Word became flesh and made His dwelling among us. We have seen His glory, the glory of the One and Only, who came from the Father, FULL of grace and truth' (author's emphasis). When the Word of Christ is taught, or preached, that word will be full of grace and truth. If the grace of Christ cannot be seen or heard in what is being taught or preached, then that particular message is not from Christ. Grace and truth are not opposites, or in any way contradictory. If they were, then Jesus Christ, being full of them both, would have been in a constant state of internal conflict – continuously seeking to balance the one against the other. The fact is that the grace of God is the truth of God, and the truth of God is the grace of God; they are one and the same – inseparable and indivisible.

The following six parables, all told by Jesus, come from the Gospel of Luke. They all show the truth of salvation by grace alone. The first five also illustrate the truth of safe-keeping through grace and the final parable shows that both salvation and empowerment for service come through grace, and grace alone.

The setting of Luke 15
Whenever a parable is taught, it is important to look at the setting within which it is being taught. The question needs to be asked, 'Why has Jesus told that story at that point to that group of people?' The correct understanding of the parable will lie in the answer to that question. To ignore the setting, that is, what is going on around Jesus at the time of the story, is to risk ending up with a story taken out of context and possibly, therefore, a story incorrectly interpreted and applied.

The background to the parables in Luke 15 is that Jesus was being accused and reviled by the Pharisees and the teachers of the Law. The reason for their accusations and revulsion was that Jesus was welcoming 'sinners' and was even eating with them. In the Middle East in the time of Jesus to eat with someone was to honour that person. To invite someone to share table fellowship was to offer peace, trust and brotherhood. Jesus is really identifying with the 'sinners' and, in effect, saying, 'I totally accept you as a brother. I am willing to sit down and have table fellowship with you.' This is a radical thing that Jesus is doing. These are not repentant sinners with whom He is dining. They are still tax collectors, possibly prostitutes, and other recognised 'sinners.' Jesus, in dining with tax collectors and 'sinners,' is making a powerful statement about God's attitude towards those whom the self-righteous reject. It was to challenge the rejection of those who were still seen as sinners that Jesus then told three parables. The first two demonstrate God's attitude to sinners and the third presents the sinner with a choice of whether or not to respond to God's gracious offer.

The lost sheep – Luke 15:1-7

Jesus opens the parable with an attack upon the prejudice and hypocrisy of the Pharisees and teachers of the Law. He says, 'Suppose one of you has a hundred sheep and loses one of them.' King David and many other Old Testament figures had been shepherds, and many prophecies speak of God acting as a shepherd for His people. Despite the apparent honoured position of shepherds in Jewish history and Scripture, the Pharisees had declared shepherds unclean. For this reason they would have been offended by Jesus' opening statement which likened them to shepherds. It was a direct challenge to their attitude to others.

Jesus goes on, 'Does he not leave the ninety-nine in the open country and go after the lost sheep until he finds it.' Jesus is beginning to explain God's attitude towards sinners. Jesus is revealing, to those who asked the question, 'Why is He eating with sinners?' just how much God cares for each and every individual, and the lengths to which God will go to find that lost sinner. Jesus uses the example of a shepherd for different reasons. One of the reasons is that a sheep when lost will sit down and not move. It will not attempt to find its way home. It is and has to be, therefore, the shepherd's responsibility to find the sheep. The shepherd has to keep searching until he finds the sheep, or the sheep will die. The shepherd is, in fact, the lost sheep's only hope of life. These are very simple but very powerful illustrations of the truth of the Gospel. God came looking for lost sinners. God will keep searching out lost sinners. He has to because He is the only hope that lost sinners have. Sinners cannot contribute anything towards altering their state of lostness. The Gospel of grace is being clearly laid out. When the sheep is found the shepherd, '... joyfully puts it on his shoulders and goes home' (Luke 15:5). This is a very important point for Christians to understand. The searching out and finding of lost sinners is God's responsibility. A lost sinner can do nothing about his lostness. When a 'sinner' becomes a Christian there is a tendency to take on the burden of ensuring one's on-going salvation; a striving to keep on the 'narrow road that leads to life' (Matt. 7:14). That striving, that fear of going astray, is the cause of endless unhappiness and division within the Christian church. Yet, in the parable of the lost sheep, Jesus is clearly teaching that it is the shepherd's responsibility to get the sheep safely back home – which, for the Christian, is the ensuring of the Christian's security for the rest of his or her life on earth. Not only is it the shepherd's responsibility but, Jesus teaches, the carrying of that burden is something He undertakes, 'joyfully.' What a wonderful message to be able to present to a struggling Christian. What Good News for the person who would become a Christian but for the fact that they know they 'could never be good enough'. The shepherd has made no demands of the sheep; but has accepted fully the consequences of the sheep becoming lost and, additionally, the responsibility for the restoration of the sheep back into its community. That is God's wonderful message of salvation to mankind. God Himself, making no demands of lost sinners, accepts fully the consequences of man's lostness and equally accepts fully the responsibility of restoring man back into communion with Himself. When a lost sinner is brought into the community of

Believers, that person is not there by their own efforts, but by God's, and the welcome and acceptance that new Believers receive should reflect that truth. When the shepherd had restored the lost sheep to the village community he called all his friends and neighbours to celebrate the finding and restoration of that lost sheep. When a lost sinner is saved, let the community of Believers celebrate – rather than looking at any apparent shortcomings that there may still be in the new Believer. Let the community of Believers allow Christ to carry the burden of the new convert, rather than sowing fears of a lost salvation over some sinful habit that may not yet have been overcome or set aside. Jesus finishes the parable by saying, 'I tell you that in the same way there will be more rejoicing in heaven over one sinner who repents than over ninety-nine righteous persons who do not need to repent' (Luke 15:7). Here Jesus is obviously likening the one lost sheep to one repentant sinner. He is beginning to reveal a new understanding of what it is to be repentant. In order to understand this new revelation of repentance, the question needs to be asked, 'What did the lost sheep do that allows Jesus to liken it to a repentant sinner?' An examination of the parable shows that the sheep, essentially, did two things. Firstly, the sheep got lost. Every Christian would accept that they too, prior to salvation, were lost. Secondly, the sheep accepted being found. The sheep allowed the shepherd to take the responsibility for restoring the sheep to its community. Jesus is here defining repentance as the acceptance of lostness and the acceptance of being found. This is entirely in keeping with the Gospel of Jesus Christ, within which the responsibility for a sinner's salvation and safe-keeping rests completely with God.

Summary
It is the shepherd who is responsible for finding the lost sheep. The parable shows that, despite all appearances to the contrary, sinners belong to God and that God wants them back and will go to great lengths to win them back. This is tremendously good news for Christian and non-Christian alike. The responsibility for restoring and maintaining communion

between God and man is God's and He willingly accepts that responsibility and resolutely carries it through to its joyful conclusion.

It is the shepherd who is responsible for the sheep's well-being even after it has been found. When the Christian is saved, he is restored into relationship with God, relationship with the Christian community and relationship with him or herself. The shepherd joyfully restores the sheep. Jesus joyfully restores the saved sinner into community. Jesus teaches that it is His joy to bear the burden of the saved Believer from the moment of salvation until the Believer enters Glory.

Lastly, there is ***a new understanding of repentance***. For the Rabbis, repentance was a condition to be met before grace could be offered. Jesus teaches that this is not the case. The sheep, and equally the sinner, does nothing to prompt the shepherd's diligent searching and restoration except to become lost and accept being found. This, then, is the new definition of repentance – the acceptance of God's work on man's behalf.

Here is a parable from Jesus which is truly, '... full of grace and truth.' A gracious message which proclaims that God, and He alone, is the One who seeks, saves and restores sinners.

The lost coin – Luke 15:8-10

Jesus continues the message of the lost sheep with this second parable. Once again Jesus starts by attacking the prejudice of the day by making, in a male-dominated society, a woman the central figure in the story. Jesus will not accept attitudes that regard any section of society as anything less than equal with all other parts of society.

A peasant village, at the time of Jesus, would be self-supporting in terms of crops, animals, skills and a system of bartering. Cash would have been quite rare, so the loss of a coin would be a serious event. Jesus is using illustrations which show the importance and value that God attaches to a lost sinner. The coin, in the village community, has a much greater value than just its face value. God sees within each person a far greater value than that which is apparent from just the outside.

This parable contains the same main points as the lost sheep. There is the grace of the thorough search, carried on relentlessly until the lost one is found. There is the joy of finding and restoring the lost coin. The cost of the search is illustrated, and is carried by the woman. Finally, Jesus likens the lost coin to a repentant sinner and, in so doing, illustrates His new definition of repentance – the acceptance of lostness and the acceptance of being found.

The lost son – Luke 15:11-24

Through lack of understanding of the culture of the Middle East at the time of Jesus there can often be misunderstanding about the message that Jesus was really teaching. This parable, for example, has become known as the Parable of the Prodigal, or Lost, Son. In fact, there are two lost sons in this parable; lost in the sense that both are out of relationship with their father. Christians are generally taught to identify with the younger son. They have lived life under their own power and direction, realised it was leading them nowhere and returned to their father. Those actually listening to Jesus would have interpreted the parable completely differently. They would have been encouraged to identify with the older son. The younger son is a complete story and, as such, requires no response from the listeners. The older son, on the other hand, is still out of relationship with his father when the story ends. The listener is supposed to identify with that older son, and decide his or her own reaction. Will he or she accept the Father's invitation back into the family – not as a servant, but as a son? This is a parable for the unbeliever, not for the Believer. It does, for the Believer, illustrate major points in Jesus' teaching and, from that point of view, it is very important; but, it requires no response from a born-again Believer. A modern understanding that the older son represents a jealous, or otherwise upset, Believer can be quickly shown to be wrong by the fact that, at the end of the story, there is no father/son relationship between the Father and the older son – clearly, the older son is unsaved at this point.

The younger son's request. The parable opens with the younger son requesting, 'Father, give me my share of the estate.' That which was due to the younger son would not come to him until his father had died. In making this request, the younger son is in effect saying, 'Look, I can't wait for you to die; I want what's mine now.' It is a stark illustration of the total breakdown in the relationship between the father and the son. In those days, the family was the most important unit within society. The listeners would have expected the older brother to have protested loudly at such a heartless request. Not only should he have strongly rebuked his younger brother, but he should also have declared that he certainly wouldn't be taking his share of the inheritance until the due time. Instead, the older brother remains perfectly silent. That silence would have had a profound meaning to Jesus' listeners showing, as it did, the equally shattered relationship between the father and the older son. The older son, by his silence, accepts the division of the estate and so receives his half, thus confirming that he too cannot wait for the father to die. The only difference between the two brothers at this point is that the younger brother has voiced his feelings, whereas the older brother has yet to do so. Within the father's response is an amazing illustration of God's love. The father had the legal right to reprimand his younger son – even to the point of having him stoned for rebellion, as laid down in the Law of Moses. Instead the father's love is sufficient even to allow for the son's rejection of his father.

The younger son's journey. After the younger son has spent all his money on wild living in a Gentile country he encounters hard times. There is a famine. Listeners to Jesus would have been familiar with famines and the disastrous effects they had. They would also have been aware of the acutely vulnerable position in which this young Jew finds himself. He is without money, without friends, a Jew in a Gentile land and that in the grip of a famine. Despite his dire circumstances, his pride is still not broken. He thinks he can sort out his problems and obtains a job – albeit, feeding pigs. Eventually the son realises that, despite trying to sort out his problems, he is still slowly starving to death.

His plan of salvation. In verse 18 of the passage he comes up with a plan. He plans, as revealed in verse 19, to go back to his father and say, 'I am no longer worthy to be called your son, make me like one of your hired men.' This is often taught, today, as repentance. As a turning around, as a going back to the father. It needs to be stated most clearly that, according to the teachings of Jesus, the younger son is entirely unrepentant at this stage. The younger son thinks that the money he has squandered, and the way he has lived, is the problem between him and his father. He has not yet realized that it is the broken relationship which is the real issue. Seeing the money as the issue, the younger son's plan is to work for his father and, out of his wages, to pay him back. Thus, the younger son is to be the author of his own salvation. That is not repentance! Additionally, as one of his father's hired men, he won't be living in the family home - because hired men do not do that. So under the younger son's plan, the split between father and son will remain. The only purpose of paying the money back is so that the younger son can return to his home village without fear of punishment either from his father or from the other villagers - who, by this time, will obviously have heard what has happened. The young man has no idea that he needs to receive grace.

The father's response. On seeing the returning son the father is filled with compassion. He runs through the village streets to meet his son. In those times no man would run in public; it would be considered undignified, even humiliating. The more stately a man's walk, the more he gained respect. The father, though, knows that the village is angry against his son. By squandering his inheritance in a Gentile land, by working as a pigherder, the young man has disgraced his whole village. The father must reach the son before any of the villagers do. This is a powerful illustration of God's love for man, and of the cross in particular. The father accepts the public humiliation brought on by running to save his son - just as Jesus later accepted the public humiliation of the cross in order to offer salvation to mankind. The father in this story, and Christ on the cross, made the reconciliation totally public. For all to see, the father hugs the son and kisses him. Nothing is held back by the father; he wants everyone to know that he is offering the son, without any conditions, any reprimand, any questions, full restoration into the family in the position of a son.

The younger son repents. The son came back with the intention of being the author of his own salvation. He came back thinking that his lifestyle and the money was the issue. He came back with the attitude of a servant, 'I will work for you.' He meets with this overwhelming demonstration of love and acceptance from the father and realises that the issue the father wants sorted out is the broken relationship – and that only the father has the right to offer restoration of that relationship. Now the son begins to realize his need to receive grace, for here is a situation which is beyond his ability to change. The son knows what it has cost the father to run through the village. He knows what it has cost the father to publicly hug and kiss him. The son then faces a decision. Does he continue with his plan to work for his father and, through his own efforts, pay back his father; or does he accept this freely offered, unconditional restoration into sonship? Is he going to repent, as Jesus teaches it, and accept being found? In verse 21 there is repentance. The son declares his unworthiness of being called a son – something all Christians can identify with – but drops his planned offer to work for his father. He accepts the position of a son which, being undeserved, is offered through grace.

Jesus is teaching here that what bothers God is the broken relationship between Him and His children. The way people live is not an issue – because Jesus has borne the penalty for all man's sins. In the story, receiving the father's love turned a would-be servant into a son. If Christians wish to know whether they have truly grasped grace, they need only ask themselves the question, 'Am I living as a servant, or as a son? Am I seeking to 'work' for God – or am I receiving the freely offered position of a son?' If there are lingering doubts within the mind of a Christian that somehow he, or she, has to 'do something' for God then that Christian needs to delve deeper into the wonders of grace. God makes no demands of any person, except faith, in terms of a person's restoration into relationship with Him.

At the end of the parable Jesus again illustrates the joy that there is in heaven when a lost sinner repents. The father kills the fatted calf and invites the whole village to join with him in this celebration of a son who 'was dead and is alive again, he was lost and is found.' This joy of restoration could not have occurred unless the son had accepted grace.

Summary. A New Covenant Believer must live under New Covenant **repentance**, as taught by Jesus, and not Old Covenant repentance which was taught by the Rabbis and which placed a heavy burden on man. Salvation is a gift, freely offered through **grace**. It is a gift which only God can offer. Man must accept his lostness, realizing that there is nothing he can do about it. God's love is freely offered and is a love that seeks and suffers in order to save. God, and the angels of heaven, share the *joy* of finding and restoring a lost sinner. A relationship with His children is God's desire. God offers **sonship**, not servanthood.

The Shrewd Manager – Luke 16:1-8

The setting and background. This parable is told by Jesus to the disciples; thus, it is a parable for the saved, not for the unsaved. It is a parable which deals with the issues of both salvation and on-going sanctification and, as such, cannot be applied to the unsaved. In the parable, the master is a wealthy land-owner with a manager who has authority to carry out the business of the estate. The debtors are almost certainly men who have rented the estate land and who have agreed to pay a fixed amount of produce for the yearly rent. The villagers have shown they respect the land owner by the fact that someone has alerted him about his dishonest manager.

The initial encounter. When the master says to the manager, 'What is this I hear about you?' the manager makes no reply. Those listening to Jesus would have expected this silence. The manager doesn't know how much the master knows; his best bet is, at this stage, to keep quiet and hope the master doesn't know too much. The master, though, then goes on and fires the manager. The manager still remains quiet. The audience would have expected the manager, now with nothing to lose, to loudly protest his innocence. In keeping quiet the manager is effectively acknowledging his guilt. The manager is also acknowledging other things through his silence; he is acknowledging that the master knows what has been going on, that he is a master who demands obedience and that he is a master who punishes disobedience. The manager has realized that there is no point offering excuses to such a master. The manager, though, has also seen another very important aspect in his master's character. Although the manager has been stealing from the master, he is not sent to jail – which the social and judicial norms of that time would have demanded. The manager has seen in this encounter two very important aspects to the master's character: one, he is a master who exacts justice and two, he is a master who tempers justice with mercy.

The manager's problem and solution. The manager now has a problem. He has lost his job and he does not know how he will survive. He eliminates various options and then comes up with a solution. His plan is to reduce the size of the debts due to the master from those who are renting his land. As the manager it is his job to negotiate these rents so he will get the credit, from the debtors, for obtaining the reductions – and that will ensure his well-being now that his job has ended. He has to act quickly before the debtors find out that he no longer has authority to reduce their rents. The manager carries out his plan and then delivers the newly altered books to his master.

The master's response. The master now has two choices. His first option is to go into the village and tell them it was all a mistake and the reductions were not valid. If he does this the debtors could become angry with him for his apparent meanness. His second option is to keep silent, absorb the losses, and receive the praise being given to him for his generosity. That praise is not unfair because the listener has already heard that the master is a generous man, and a merciful man – shown by his dealing with his manager. The master's reaction is to compliment the manager on his shrewdness. In the *RSV* the master says, 'You are a wise fellow.' One of the Old Testament definitions of wisdom is 'the instinct for self-preservation.' In the Old Testament 'wisdom' is also used to mean 'cleverness.' It is in this context that the master compliments the manager. The master is, in effect, saying, 'Well done. You were clever enough to see where you only hope of self-preservation lay, and you took it.' The master is complimenting the manager, not for his dishonesty, but for his instinct for survival which lay behind his plan. The master thus becomes the instrument of the manager's initial salvation – in that he did not send the manager to jail – and he then becomes the instrument of the manager's on-going salvation, or sanctification, by absorbing the cost of the manager's repeated dishonesty.

The disciples – and Christians today – are being encouraged by Jesus to have the same daring hope in God's mercy and generosity. Daring to believe that the same grace which initially saves will, also, eternally ensure the Believer's well-being.

Summary. The manager was a sinner – as is man. The manager had received his master's mercy – as has the Christian. The manager had no means of providing for his own future well-being; just as, despite being saved, the Christian cannot then keep right with God by his own efforts. The manager entrusted his future well-being to his master's on-going mercy; the Christian is encouraged by Jesus to do likewise. The master commended the manager for seeing where his only hope of well-being lay, and for his shrewdness in then resting all of his hope on the on-going mercy of the master. Jesus is teaching that the Christian is, far from taking advantage of God's mercy, being equally shrewd in resting all of his or her hope on God's on-going mercy.

The good Samaritan – Luke 10:25-37

This is a parable which has been greatly mistaught over the years. It is a parable that is often taught as an encouragement to go out and do good works. The reason for this misteaching is that the parable is long and the conversation around it is short. The consequence of this is that the conversation is often over-looked. Yet, as has already been written, in order to get a correct interpretation of a parable it is necessary to look at the circumstances that surround the telling of the parable. Both the short conversations that take place before the parable itself start by stating the motive of the lawyer.

The first conversation. In the first question the lawyer puts to Jesus the motive is to test Jesus. The Pharisees and the teachers of the Law had a problem with Jesus. He didn't seem to stick to the

Law in the way that He, according to their understanding, should do. Jesus healed on the Sabbath, His disciples picked and ate corn on the Sabbath, neither He nor His disciples fasted and neither He nor His disciples observed aspects of the ceremonial law. These were all issues upon which the Jewish religious authorities had criticized Jesus. The lawyer, then, has come to test Jesus on His attitude to the Law - did He uphold it or not? The lawyer asked the question, 'What must I do to inherit eternal life?' The reason the lawyer asks this question is because the Rabbis taught that if a person obeyed the Law then that person would inherit eternal life - in other words, a person could earn their salvation. Jesus, knowing the teaching of the time, knows that the lawyer will see obedience to the Law as the way of inheriting eternal life, so He asks the lawyer his own understanding of the requirements of the Law. Jesus asks the lawyer, 'What is written in the Law?' The lawyer's response is to quote Jesus' teaching that the requirement of the Law is to love 'God with all your heart, with all your soul, with all your strength and with all your mind and to love your neighbour as yourself'. Jesus tells the lawyer that he has answered correctly. Now, though, the lawyer has a problem. He had asked Jesus for a limited requirement, based upon the Law, that he might obey in order to inherit eternal life; instead the answer which he himself gives is a command that requires unlimited and unreserved love for God and for people. The very Law the lawyer turns to sets a standard that no person can reach.

The second conversation. The lawyer then asks his second question and this time his motive is to justify himself. In other words, he is still looking for self-justification. Having seen, as a result of his first question, a standard in the Law that he cannot reach, he now asks Jesus to narrow down the requirement to a level that the lawyer will be able to meet. 'And who is my neighbour?' he asks. This is a very reasonable question because, under Jewish law, Gentiles were certainly not considered neighbours. Equally, Samaritans were not considered neighbours to the Jews.

This lawyer will be expecting to hear something along the lines of, 'Your fellow Jew is your neighbour.'

It is to answer these questions about the means of justification that Jesus then tells the parable. By understanding this it can be seen that the meaning of the parable will revolve around the means of justification, and will not be an encouragement to do good works.

The robbery. The person who was robbed was left stripped and half-dead. What the robbers leave at the roadside is not a Jew, not a Samaritan, not a Gentile; but just a man. He cannot be identified by national or local dress styles because he has been stripped. He cannot speak to identify himself because he is 'half-dead.' The Jews had different phrases for stages of death and 'half-dead' means that the man was unconscious and unable to communicate. Anyone coming upon this man would have no way of knowing whether he was Jew or Gentile. Equally, anyone coming upon the man would have no way of knowing how close he was to death.

The priest. Under Jewish law the priest had a legal right to pass this man by. The priest risked becoming 'unclean' by contact with the man if he turned out to be a Gentile. The priest also risked becoming 'unclean' if he touched the man and found him to be dead. So the listeners to Jesus would not have been surprised that the priest 'passed by on the other side.' In fact, they would have been very surprised if the priest had done anything else.

The Levite. The Levite is following the priest. Although the Levite is not bound by as many rules as the priest, his problem is that if he goes to the aid of the injured man then he, the Levite, may be seen to be suggesting that the priest's interpretation of the Law was wrong. The Levite could reasonably assume that the priest would have helped the man if there had been a legal need to do so. Again, those listening to Jesus would not have been at all surprised by the actions of the Levite who also, 'passed by on the other side.'

Jewish/Samaritan relationships. This story is being told only a few years after some Samaritans desecrated the Temple in Jerusalem by throwing human bones into it. Relationships between the two communities were at an all-time low. The listeners to Jesus would have been expecting a Jewish layman to be the hero of His story but, to their surprise, Jesus then introduces a hated Samaritan as the next person in the parable.

The Samaritan. The Samaritan is bound by the same Torah as the priest and the Levite. The attack has taken place between Jerusalem and Jericho, which is in Judea; so the chances of the wounded man being a neighbour, that is a fellow Samaritan, are nil. As the Samaritan is travelling through Judea, on his way to Samaria, it can be fairly easily established that he is probably a trader. He is certainly riding on a donkey and can, therefore, be shown to be relatively well-off. He is a prime target for the robbers if they are still in the vicinity. So the very act of stopping puts the Samaritan at risk. Jewish Law, giving as it did the right of retaliation, also puts the Samaritan at risk. This is because the Jews, due to the state of Jewish/Samaritan relationships at that time, would have assumed that it was Samaritan robbers who had attacked the wounded Jew. The wounded man's family may well, therefore, have reacted violently against the Samaritan. Despite the very real dangers to himself the Samaritan feels a deep compassion for the wounded man – a compassion which is immediately translated into action; and it is here that the reader/listener can begin to detect the role of God with mankind.

The Messianic comparison. The Samaritan is in no way responsible for what has happened to the wounded man, yet he compensates for all that has happened to him. The Samaritan compensates for the lack of compassion of both the priest and the Levite and he compensates for the robbers – they robbed the man, the Samaritan pays for him (at the inn). All the others, in one way or another, abandon the man; the Samaritan takes him to the inn and sees that he is taken care of. It costs the Samaritan time, money, effort and risk of personal danger. The Samaritan is a totally unknown stranger, yet despite the costs and the dangers he freely demonstrates unexpected, unconditional and unlimited love to the one in need. The Samaritan illustrates the mission of Jesus in that he is an unexpected source of salvation, comes to heal, save and restore, accepts possible misunderstanding and hostility and pays the price himself for salvation and restoration.

The meaning of the parable. The parable is NOT an

encouragement to do good works for one's neighbour. The parable is told within the context of a conversation about self-justification. Jesus answers the lawyer's questions about self-justification by showing the standard God requires from those who would seek to be right with Him. In doing so, Jesus reveals a standard that is beyond reach. The problem for the lawyer, and for all people, is that God's standard is beyond reach. Jesus is pointing out, not the need for good works, but the need every human being has of a Saviour.

The two debtors – Luke 7:40-43

The setting. Once again, the context within which this parable is told gives the key to the correct understanding of what Jesus is seeking to teach. This short parable is set within a longer story of an event which actually happened. Jesus has been invited to the house of Simon the Pharisee. Upon entry, Jesus is subject to a series of calculated insults – these are set out in verses 44-46. The reason for these insults is given when Simon reveals, through his thinking in verse 39, that his motive in inviting Jesus to his house was to make his own assessment as to whether or not Jesus was a prophet. The woman, in the sequence of events makes up for Simon's lack of hospitality. It is these contrasting actions that lead to the parable.

The parable. This is a short but very powerful parable. In it Jesus, once again, teaches that before God all are equal. The two debtors in the story are made equal by the fact that both are in debt and neither can do anything to alter that situation. Both, no matter the size of their individual debt, are dependent upon the mercy of the one to whom they are in debt. There is a great lesson here for all Christians. All Christians are equal in the sight of God. All Christians are totally dependent upon God's mercy. There is great potential for unity within Christianity when Christians truly understand the total dependence of all Believers upon God.

Simon's response. Although Simon has completely misread the actions of Jesus and the woman, he is able to see, through the parable, that the response to undeserved grace is love – and a love that enables and empowers acts of service. The greater the grace, the greater the response. This is such a powerful message for all Believers. As Christians receive grace Jesus teaches, far from slipping into slovenly spiritual habits and an abuse of grace, that very receiving of grace will empower the Believer.

The theme. God's freely offered love, accepted as undeserved grace, is the theme of the parable. Forgiveness is a freely offered gift of God. Salvation is by faith alone. When accepted, this salvation by faith triggers acts of service which, as in this case, may be costly. These acts of service, the Believer's love response to God's love, are expressions of thanks for grace, and forgiveness received, not attempts to gain more of either.

Conclusion

The Bible says, as expressed at the beginning of this chapter, that Jesus came, '. . . full of grace and truth.' These parables illustrate the truth of that Scripture; the teachings of Jesus are, indeed, full of grace and truth. These parables show that grace saves, heals, restores and empowers. When receiving teaching or preaching upon the Gospel of Christ, the listener should search for the grace in the message; if it is not there, then that message should be set aside as one which is not in keeping with the teachings of Jesus. In this way, the Believer will protect him or herself from taking on a burden which is not from God. Every Believer should follow the command of Scripture, in Colossians 4:6, and should 'Let your conversation be always full of grace, seasoned with salt, so that you may know how to answer everyone.' Jesus Christ - full of grace and truth; may all Believers follow His example and faithfully teach His message of Good News.

CHAPTER 5

Grace Scriptures

The following is a look at what the New Testament says, in depth, on the subject of grace. A verse or two taken in isolation, on any subject, can lead to a distortion of understanding of that subject. This look at the grace Scriptures of the New Testament gives an overview of the whole subject.

John 1:14 **'The Word became flesh and made His dwelling among us. We have seen His glory, the glory of the One and Only, who came from the Father, full of grace and truth.'** Jesus came FULL of grace and truth. The two are inseparable. God's grace is God's truth. God's truth is God's grace. When something, or someone, is FULL of something then there is no room for anything else.

John 1:16 **'From the fullness of His grace we have all received one blessing after another.'** In the New Covenant, blessings are freely given through God's grace - they are not earned, as under the Old Covenant. As it is grace which brings the blessings, then a Christian's fruit, or otherwise, can in no way affect his relationship with God or the blessings received from Him.

John 1:17 **'For the Law came through Moses; grace and truth came through Jesus Christ.'**

Jesus did not bring the same message as Moses. The Law pointed out man's need for a Saviour. Jesus came as that Saviour. Jesus did not come to reinforce the Law; He came to fulfil and then abolish it.

Acts 6:8 **'Now Stephen, a man full of God's grace and power, did great wonders and miraculous signs among the people.'**

Grace and power go together. Grace is not an easy option or an alternative to obedience - it is always taught as being the very source of power and obedience in a Believer's life. To embrace grace is to embrace God's power to live the life into which He has called the Believer.

Acts 15:10-11 **'Now then, why do you try to test God by putting on the necks of the disciples a yoke that neither we nor our fathers have been able to bear? No! We believe it is through the grace of our Lord Jesus that we are saved, just as they are.'**

From the very beginning of the Church, people have been confused about where the Law fits into a Believer's life now that grace has appeared. In these verses Peter is confronting just that situation in Jerusalem, where some were saying that new Believers had to pay attention to the Law of Moses. Peter firmly rejects that idea and affirms that it is by grace that people are saved.

Romans 1:5 **'Through Him and for His name's sake, we received grace and apostleship to call people from among all the Gentiles to the obedience that comes from faith.'**

Paul received grace and, through that, apostleship and was thus enabled to call people to Christ. Believers today should follow Paul's example – receive grace and, through that, empowerment for service. Note, also, that Paul called Believers to an obedience that came from faith, not from constant striving.

Romans 3:23-24 **'For all have sinned and fall short of the glory of God, and are justified freely by His grace through the redemption that came by Christ Jesus.'**

FREE justification! Christians don't earn it, deserve it, contribute towards it or pay for it. It is free. It is by grace. Justified – 'just as if I'd' never sinned – and it's free.

Romans 5:1-2 **'Therefore, since we have been justified by faith, we have peace with God through our Lord Jesus Christ, through whom we have gained access by faith into this grace in which we now stand.'**

A Christian can enter into grace through faith, daring to believe that despite the way he lives, he is OK with God. Christians stand in grace. Grace empowers.

Romans 5:17 **'... how much more will those who receive God's abundant provision of grace and of the gift of**

righteousness reign in life through the one man, Jesus Christ.'

There is only one way to reign in life, only one way to know and live in the victory of Jesus Christ, and that is to receive the abundant grace which God freely offers. Receive grace freely and reign – or try and be worthy of it, or earn it, and live in continual defeat.

Romans 5:20 **'The law was added so that the trespass might increase. But where sin increased, grace increased all the more.'**

The purpose of the Law was to highlight sin – in order that man should see his need for a Saviour. As a person becomes more aware of sin in his life, so it makes that person ever more dependent upon God's grace. Sin should not separate a Christian from God, but should drive the Christian ever closer to Him to receive the grace which is needed – and which is so freely offered.

Romans 6:14 **'For sin shall not be your master, because you are not under law, but under grace.'**

The answer to the burden of sin is grace. Live under grace, says this Scripture, and sin shall not be the master. The Bible tells why this is so. 1 Cor. 15:56 says, 'The power of sin is the Law.' Take away the Law and, thus, take away sin's power. The Believer is called to live not under the Law but under grace and, therefore, released from the power of sin.

Romans 11:5-6 **'So too, at the present time there is a remnant chosen by grace. And if by grace, then it is no longer by works; if it were, grace would no longer be grace.'**

Chosen by grace. Praise God! But grace must be free or it is not grace. All a person can do with grace is gratefully receive it.

1 Cor. 1:3 **'Grace and peace to you from God our Father and the Lord Jesus Christ.'**

Here grace and peace are linked. When Christians are robbed of their peace it is because they have allowed themselves to come under Law in their thinking and, perhaps, their living. Romans 5:1 says, '. . . we have peace with God through our Lord Jesus Christ.' If Christians come to God the Father through Jesus then they have peace with God. So if Christians are not experiencing peace it must be because they are seeking to come to God in some way other than Jesus. That 'other way' is always their own efforts, their own lifestyle. Jesus said, 'Peace I give you . . .' The world can give people peace BECAUSE of their lifestyle – escapism, comfort, relationships, wealth; but Jesus, and He alone, gives a Christian that inner peace DESPITE their lifestyle.

***1 Cor. 15:10* 'But by the grace of God I am what I am, and His grace to me was not without effect. No, I worked harder than all of them – yet not I, but the grace of God that was with me.'**

Paul says here that it was receiving grace that empowered him to do all that he did in the service of the GospeL Grace is often seen as an easy option – an alternative to obedience; the truth of this, and similar Scriptures, is the complete opposite. Grace is, in fact, the very source of power and obedience in a Christian's life. If a Christian wishes to be productive for Christ, and for the Gospel, that Christian should receive grace – that is the Word of God.

***2 Cor. 4:15* 'All this is for your benefit, so that the grace that is reaching more and more people may cause thanksgiving to overflow to the glory of God.'**

Grace causes thanksgiving to overflow in the life of a Christian – and that brings glory to God. Grace makes a Christian grateful to God for what He has done, and that gratitude leads to service – grace-inspired, grace-empowered service.

***2 Cor. 9:8* 'And God is able to make all grace abound to you, so that in all things at all times, having all that you need, you will abound in every good work.'**

Another Scripture that points to grace as the source of power and service in the life of a Christian. Christian service, as with all things in the Gospel, is the responsibility of God. He makes grace abound, He equips the Christian with 'all that you need' in order that the Christian may, thus empowered, 'abound in every good work.'

***2 Cor. 12:9* 'But He said, "My grace is sufficient for you . . . " '**

'Sufficient' means lacking nothing. Having all that is needed.

These words of Christ reassure the Christian that, in all circumstances, Christ's grace lacks nothing in its ability to meet the Christian's every need. Such is the power of grace – whatever the need, grace meets it. What is the need? Forgiveness, freedom, empowerment, victory, love? Grace, upon the promise of Jesus Himself, will meet the need. Let every Christian receive it.

Gal. 2:21 **'I do not set aside the grace of God, for if righteousness could be gained through the law, Christ died for nothing.'**

If there is any other way to achieve righteousness, other than through Christ's death, then Christ died for nothing. That is the uncompromising message of Paul. Let every Believer today receive the 'gift of righteousness' that God offers through Jesus (Rom. 5:17), let all striving and legalism cease and let every Believer begin to live in the peace with God which Jesus, and He alone, can give (Rom. 5:1).

Gal. 3:18 **'For if the inheritance depends on the law, then it no longer depends on grace; but God in His grace gave it to Abraham through a promise.'**

The Christian's inheritance depends upon grace. This means that not only is the Christian saved by grace, but that the Christian is also kept safe by grace – ready to receive the inheritance at the right time. Understanding this removes a great burden from the Christian and places the Christian's eternal destiny squarely in the hands of God. Such Good News allows the Christian to relax, live in the joy of their salvation and enjoy a deeper and more stable relationship with God their Father.

Eph. 1:4-6 **'For He chose us in Him before the creation of the world to be holy and blameless in His sight. In love He predestined us to be adopted as His sons through Jesus Christ, in accordance with His pleasure and will – to the praise of His glorious grace which He has freely given us in the One He loves.'**

What a Scripture! Chosen before the world was created. Holy and blameless in the sight of God. Predestined as sons. And all through His gift of grace – Jesus. What security, what joy, what peace belong to the Christian who accepts this Scripture.

Eph. 1:7 **'In Him we have redemption through His blood, the forgiveness of sins, in accordance with the riches of God's grace that He lavished on us with all wisdom and understanding.'**

Redeemed by the blood of Jesus. Forgiveness for our sins, through God's grace. The focus in the Gospel is always on what God has done for man. Christians become unstable when the focus becomes what they should be doing for God. And God knew what He was doing when He poured out His grace and forgave man's sins – He did that with all His wisdom and understanding

Eph. 2:4-5 **'But because of His great love for us God, who is rich in mercy, made us alive with Christ even when we were dead in transgressions – it is by grace you have been saved.'**

'... because of His great love ...' – that is why Christians were made alive in Christ, it had nothing to do, whatsoever, with the Christian's efforts. It is by grace that Christians have been saved The focus of the Good News doesn't ever change from God's efforts on man's behalf.

Eph. 2:6-7 **'And God raised us up with Christ and seated us with Him in the heavenly realms in Christ Jesus, in order that in the coming ages He might show the incomparable riches of His grace, expressed in His kindness to us in Christ Jesus.'**

God has raised Christians up for a purpose. The purpose is that for all eternity they will be a demonstration of God's amazing grace. In receiving God's grace Christians are perfectly in line with God's will. Receive and rejoice, and let all creation marvel at the greatness of God's grace.

Eph. 2:8-9 **'For it is by grace you have been saved, through faith – and this not from yourselves, it is the gift of God – not by works, so that no-one can boast.'**

Christians contribute nothing to their salvation. Christians are saved by grace, entering into grace through faith (Rom. 5:2) and that faith, as this Scripture says, is the gift of God. Salvation is a work of God for man from beginning to end. A Christian's lifestyle neither adds to, nor takes away from, the work that God has done on man's behalf.

Col. 1:6 'All over the world this gospel is bearing fruit and growing, just as it has been doing among you since the day you heard it and understood God's grace in all its truth.'

The Gospel will grow and bear fruit - once it has been heard and the grace of God fully understood. This Scripture shows that understanding grace helps the spread and effectiveness of the Gospel. Christians should never listen to teaching that places a limit on how much to embrace grace - such teaching could not be more wrong. Embracing grace does not lead to licence, but to growth and fruit.

Col. 4:6 'Let your conversation be always full of grace, seasoned with salt, so that you may know how to answer everyone.'

Christians should always be talking about grace - that is the instruction from this verse of Scripture. Christians should talk it, preach it, teach it, live it. To be 'full' of something is to have no room for anything else. Christians should have no room for anything but grace. That is not an out of balance approach - it is a Biblical approach. 'Seasoned with salt' should not be interpreted to mean that there should be limits placed upon grace. Salt is a preservative. The message is that Christians should let their conversation be full of grace and that they should keep the grace message pure and fully preserved. Only in that way can Christians be effective witnesses, knowing 'how to answer everyone.'

2 Thess. 2:16 '... God our Father; who loved us and by His grace gave us eternal encouragement and good hope...'

Once again the importance of grace. It is through God's grace that Christians can receive encouragement and hope. Apart from grace, there is only the Law and a Christian's own efforts. Both are frequently sources of discouragement and lack of hope. That is why it is vital to receive grace and, through that, to receive encouragement and receive hope.

2 Tim. 1:9 'God, who has saved us and called us to a holy life – not because of anything we have done but because of

His own purpose and grace. This grace was given us in Christ Jesus before the beginning of time . . . '

How could it be any more plain? Christians are saved, but 'NOT BECAUSE OF ANYTHING WE HAVE DONE.' It is so clear that Christians are saved because of God's actions on man's behalf. There is little point God saving Christians if He then expects them to maintain their salvation by their own efforts. It is clear that the Christian is saved by grace and is kept saved by grace. Saved means SAVED! It doesn't mean temporarily rescued. It doesn't mean saved subject to certain conditions or subject to a certain standard of living. Saved by grace means exactly what it says.

This grace was given before time began. All man needs to do is receive it, not earn it or seek to in some way be worthy of it. When God gave His grace before time began He was perfectly aware of how Christians would live after they were saved. He knew that they would not suddenly start living sinless lives out of gratitude for what He had done. He knew how they would respond once they were saved. That's part of His amazing grace, that despite knowing that, He still chose to save the Christian!

2 Tim. 2:1 'You then, my son, be strong in the grace that is in Christ Jesus.'

Grace is the source of strength in a Christian's life. If a Christian is feeling spiritually weak it will be because they have looked away from the amazing grace which they have been freely given. This is a grace which can set a fire in a Christian's spirit, can melt hearts, set wills for God and set the Christian against sin. Grace is never revealed as anything other than the very source of strength by which Christians overcome and live holy lives.

Titus 2:11-12 'For the grace of God that brings salvation has appeared to all men. It teaches us to say "No" to ungodliness and worldly passions, and to live self-controlled, upright and godly lives in this present age . . . '

The first thing to note about this Scripture is that the grace has appeared to all men. No-one is excluded. Secondly, it is the grace of God which brings salvation. It is yet another Scripture which turns man completely away from himself and towards God. This same grace then teaches the Believer the way in which to live. It doesn't demand, it teaches. Teaching is a process which takes time. This verse encourages the Christian who may feel that he isn't making much progress. 2 Peter 1:3 says that God, '... has given us everything we need for life and godliness...' Titus 2:11 tells what it is that God has given – it is grace. Grace that brings salvation, grace that brings sanctification.

Titus 3:7 **'... having been justified by His grace, we might become heirs having the hope of eternal life.'**

Justified by grace. Nowhere in Scripture is man pointed to himself when it comes to his standing before God. It is entirely a work of God for man. A holy God demands holiness. Who but God can achieve that? Man may strive, but his very best efforts will count for nothing. Christians stand before God because of grace. Let every Christian receive this grace and live in the God-given relationship.

Hebrews 4:16 **'Let us then approach the throne of grace with confidence, so that we may receive mercy and find grace to help us in our time of need.'**

What is the confidence spoken of in this verse? Confidence in man's efforts? Never! Confidence in God's grace. The verses earlier in Hebrews 4 have taught how Jesus understands human weaknesses. So Christians can be confident of God's grace despite their weaknesses; confident of His grace because of their weaknesses. It is as Christians confidently come to God in their weakness that they receive the help needed, through the grace that He extends.

Hebrews 10:29 **'How much more severely do you think a man deserves to be punished who has trampled the Son of God under foot, who has treated as an unholy thing the blood of the covenant that sanctified him, and who has insulted the Spirit of grace.'**

The Spirit of grace is insulted by only one thing: the idea that grace is insufficient. Many Christians are frightened by this verse and see it as a reference to their continuing struggles. Quite the opposite! It is a verse which points away from works. Christians are saved entirely by grace, through the blood of Jesus. Accept that, set aside striving and do not seek to add to grace.

Hebrews 13:9 **'Do not be carried away with all kinds of strange teachings. It is good for our hearts to be strengthened by grace, not by ceremonial foods which are of no value to those who eat them.'**

Feeling weak? Then let the Christian heart be strengthened – by grace. When feeling discouraged, battle-weary, a sense of failure or any other of the ills that assail the Christian – that is when to come to the throne of grace (Heb. 4:16), because it is there that strengthening is received. It is there that empowerment is received to press on, to not give up but to have peace in our hearts in the midst of the battles and even the defeats. Legalism, which is what the 'ceremonial foods' represent, is not good for Christians. It is living under the Law which weakens the Christian; grace strengthens. Grace overcomes weaknesses in a way that striving cannot.

James 4:6 **'But He gives us more grace. That is why the Scripture says, "God opposes the proud but gives grace to the humble."'**

Why is grace given to the humble and not to the proud? Because pride is naturally self-centred and self-reliant. The proud person is not aware of his need for grace and, consequently, is not open to receiving it. Humility, with its recognition of dependence upon God, brings grace which, in turn, brings freedom and power.

1 Peter 1:2 **'Grace and peace be yours in abundance.'**

A generous God! Abundant grace, abundant peace. Grace and peace are very interlinked. Peace with God in a Christian's heart, without grace, is not truly possible.

1 Peter 1:10 **'Concerning this salvation, the prophets, who spoke of the grace that was to come to you, searched intently and with the greatest care.'**

Salvation was always going to be by grace. There was never any intention that man would be saved by obedience. The prophets of old knew that and searched for the grace that was to be revealed. The prophets spoke out a message they didn't fully understand – in terms of 'time and circumstances' – and that is the situation with many Christians today. They know they are saved by grace but haven't fully understood, 'the sufferings of Christ and the glories that would follow.' Christians need to ensure that they are totally dependent upon grace, and grace alone, for their right standing before God.

1 Peter 1:13 'Therefore, prepare your minds for action; be self-controlled; set your hope fully on the grace to be given you when Jesus Christ is revealed.'

If hope is set on anything other than grace, then that hope – and a Christian's daily walk with God – will be like a seesaw. Christians have a sure and certain hope because it is rooted in what Jesus has done. To enjoy this hope, and to live in this hope, Christians must set their hope FULLY upon the grace to be given them. If Christians ever experience lack of hope, they need only turn and fix their eyes firmly on God's mighty grace – personified in Jesus – given before the beginning of time, and guaranteeing them all the riches of heaven at Christ's expense.

1 Peter 4:10 'Each one should use whatever gift he has received to serve others, faithfully administering God's grace in all its various forms.'

God's gifts to the Christian are an expression of His grace. He graciously gives these gifts in order that Christians may serve each other. So grace is again seen as the source of power in the life of the Christian. God is not impressed with the service of the Christian – because God is the One who has enabled and empowered that service. This is Good News because it means the Christian can relax and let God carry the responsibility for how the Christian serves. Such understanding removes any tendency to struggle and strive.

1 Peter 5:12 'With the help of Silas . . . I have written to you briefly, encouraging you and testifying that this is the true grace of God. Stand fast in it.'

Christians stand fast in grace. It is so important that Christians understand the power which grace brings into their lives. Christians will never stand fast in their own strength and efforts. This Scripture contains a simple command: Stand fast in grace. If a Christian is not standing fast then he or she should ask themselves what they are relying on to get through each situation – their strength, or God's grace.

2 Peter 1:2 **'Grace and peace be yours in abundance through the knowledge of God and of Jesus our Lord.'**

Again a testimony to abundant grace and peace, and once again they are linked. Here, though, there is an instruction on how to receive this abundant provision – it is '. . . through the knowledge of God and of Jesus our Lord.' Time spent in the Scriptures and in prayer will increase a Christian's knowledge of God, and so increase the grace and peace received. More time in God's presence will achieve a lot more than all a Christian's extra striving and effort.

2 Peter 3:18 **'But grow in the grace and knowledge of our Lord and Saviour Jesus Christ.'**

True Christian growth. Many would measure their growth as a Christian in terms of the sense of victory and overcoming which they are experiencing. Here the standard is shown to be 'grace and knowledge.' The marvel is that as a Christian grows in grace, and in his knowledge of Jesus Christ, so he lives out more of Christ's victory in his life. Once again the focus of the Christian is Jesus – His grace, what He has done, what He is still doing, what He is going to do, His character, His compassion, His understanding and so on. As a Christian grows in his knowledge of Jesus, so he changes. That's real growth.

Revelation 22:21 **'The *grace* of the Lord Jesus Christ be with God's people. Amen'** (author's emphasis).

Amen and amen!

PART TWO – **MORE CHRISTIAN DOCTRINE**

CHAPTER 6

'Repent and believe...'

Introduction
The Gospel, the Good News, of Jesus Christ is summed up in the words of Jesus, in Mark 1:15, when the Lord says, 'Repent and believe the good news.' This is a call that is repeated in the other Gospels. For people to see how that phrase sums up the Good News it is necessary for them to understand what the Lord was saying when He called on people to repent and, equally important, it is necessary to understand what it is that people are called to believe.

The necessity for understanding can be seen when it is realised that the word 'repent' has well over 40 different applications, according to Strong's Exhaustive Concordance. These include such diverse meanings as 'to circumcise,' 'to turn back,' 'to pervert,' 'to slide back' and 'to rejoice.' All these circumstances, and a host of others, are all covered by the use of the one word 'repent.' The purpose of this chapter is to focus upon, and answer, the fundamental question, 'What did Jesus mean when He called upon people to repent?' What does repentance, as Jesus teaches it, mean in terms of a person's relationship with God? The second purpose of this chapter is to clarify exactly what it is that a Christian should believe.

Old Testament repentance
Repentance is not a New Covenant concept. It is important to understand Old Testament, and therefore Old Covenant, repentance in order to be able to contrast it with New Testament, New Covenant repentance. In the Old Testament (Old Covenant):

The Rabbis taught Israel that **repentance was something which man initiated** and to which God then gave a warm, loving response. In Job 34:33 the question is asked, 'Should God then reward you on your terms, when you refuse to repent?' In other words, repentance was first carried out by man before the loving reward was given by God. The Rabbis taught that **repentance would restore communion with God**. Jeremiah 15:19 says, 'This is what the Lord says,"If you repent I will restore you that you may serve Me."' Here is God Himself saying that repentance will bring restoration into a relationship whereby a person may serve the Lord. Once again this puts the emphasis upon man. Man must first repent before the Lord will restore the relationship.

In the Old Testament, **repentance was an often repeated event**. Over and over again, throughout the writings of the prophets, Israel was called upon to repent because she had strayed from the ways of the Lord. Israel would be called to **repent by renouncing sin and turning back to God**.

A lack of repentance often brought hard times, or punishment. In Hosea 11:5, speaking of Israel, the question is put, 'Will they not return to Egypt and will not Assyria rule over them because they refuse to repent?' If Israel refused to repent, God was prepared to go to the extreme of allowing Israel to be overcome by her enemies.

There are other elements to Old Testament, Old Covenant, repentance. There is the element of feeling sorry for any sins committed and the element of reparation - where any wrong committed had to be put right with the person against whom the wrong had been committed. These aspects of repentance, and all the others, firmly put the emphasis upon man. Unmistakably, in the Old Testament, under the Old Covenant, repentance was something which man initiated and to which God then responded or, as in the case of Hosea, man failed to initiate and God then punished the unrepentant sinner or nation.

Some modern, and incorrect, teachings on repentance

Many Believers are taught, and hold onto, an Old Testament, Old Covenant, understanding of repentance. For many New Covenant Believers today, repentance is still something which is man-initiated, something man does to draw a response from God, something repeatedly carried out, a feeling of being and/or saying sorry, something which involves a commitment to strive to never commit a particular sin again and something which includes paying back or making up for the wrong done. Modern, and incorrect, teaching also includes that the failure to repent may be responsible for some problem or hard time being encountered by a Believer. The Christian Church is living with an essentially man-centred understanding and practice of repentance.

This wrong teaching is one area where many a Believer has been robbed of the joy of their salvation. This wrong teaching results in repentance becoming a burden to the Believer. It deflects the Believer's gaze from the cross of Christ and refocuses the Believer upon his or her own performance and, generally, his or her own inadequacies. Such a teaching brings no glory to Jesus. I have had someone say to me that he had done something wrong and that he had 'been repenting furiously ever since.' By this the person meant that he had been trying to convince God that he was truly sorry and that he would strive not to repeat that particular sin. He has, in common with many, an idea of repentance which focuses totally upon his effort and his, in some way, making himself once again acceptable to God in order to have communion restored.

The Good News of the Gospel is that it is ALL about what God, in Jesus, has done for the Believer and at no point should that emphasis ever be reversed into what the Believer does for God. One of the things which God has done for the Believer is to eternally reconcile the Believer, through Jesus, to Himself. That reconciliation is through Jesus and by Jesus – and nothing can interrupt it. This is expressed in 2 Corinthians 5:18-19, 'All this [the doing away with the old and the coming of the new in the Believer] is from God, who reconciled us to Himself through

Christ and has given us the ministry of reconciliation: that God was reconciling the world to Himself in Christ, not counting men's sins against them.'

Salvation and repentance

The Gospel affirms that salvation is by faith alone. In approximately 150 passages of the New Testament, salvation is said to depend on 'believing' or 'faith' alone. There are, though, some passages which appear to cause confusion within the Church, and within individual Believers, as to the source and means of salvation. To faith is often added the need to confess sins. This is based upon 1 John 1:9, 'If we confess our sins, He is faithful and just and will forgive us our sins and purify us from all unrighteousness.' The emphasis is usually put on the word, 'If' with the implication that if the Believer does not confess his or her sins then those sins are not forgiven. Salvation can be made dependent upon confession of Christ. In Romans 10:9 Paul writes, 'That if you confess with your mouth, "Jesus is Lord" and believe in your heart that God raised Him from the dead, you will be saved.' That Scripture is often misused to suggest that if a Christian does not openly confess Christ with his mouth then that Christian will not be saved. Baptism is another requirement which has been added to faith. This is based upon the words of Peter in Acts 2:38 when, in response to the question from the convicted Jews, 'Brothers, what shall we do?' Peter replied, 'Repent and be baptized, every one of you, in the name of Jesus Christ so that your sins may be forgiven.' In Mark 16:16 the words of Jesus Himself are, 'whoever believes and is baptized will be saved . . .'

Such Scriptures need to be read and understood in the light of the cross of Calvary. Any addition to faith alone, as the means of salvation, is to deny the sufficiency of the cross and, as such, is a message which strikes at the very heart of the Gospel. Whether that addition to faith is confession of sin, confession of Christ, baptism or repentance – or indeed, anything else – and whether that addition APPEARS to have Scriptural authority, the fundamental truth of the Christian Gospel is that faith in Christ's achievement on the cross for the Believer, and that alone, is all sufficient for salvation. 'For it is by grace you have been saved, through faith – and this not of yourselves, it is the gift of God...' Eph. 2:8.

Despite this fundamental truth of salvation by grace, through faith, the Christian cannot deny that repentance is a basic theme of the Gospels and that Jesus Christ commands His followers to repent. This, then, raises a question. Is it actually necessary to add repentance to faith as the vehicle of salvation or, under the New Covenant, is it possible that repentance is an integral part of faith and not at all a separate issue? If the latter is true, if faith and repentance inevitably go hand in hand under the New Covenant, then it removes from the individual Christian the burden of repentance – because faith, and therefore repentance, is a gift from God. If repentance is an integral part of faith – in other words, if there cannot be faith without repentance and there cannot be repentance without faith – it puts the responsibility squarely back onto God, as Ephesians 2:8 highlights. If this is the case then it brings repentance back into line with the rest of the Good News of the Gospel in which the entire emphasis is upon what God, in Jesus, has done for man.

New Testament repentance

One of the first Scriptures worth noting from the New Testament, concerning repentance, is Acts 5:31. This says, 'God exalted Him [Jesus] to His own right hand as Prince and Saviour that He might give repentance and forgiveness of sins to Israel.' The first reference to repentance outside the Gospels does, indeed, speak of repentance being a gift from God to man. In this Scripture it clearly shows that God is the initiator of New Covenant repentance – in stark contrast to the repentance of the Old Testament, Old Covenant.

Acts 11:18 emphasises the point that New Covenant repentance is initiated by God when it says, 'When they heard this [that the Holy Spirit had been given to the Gentiles], they had no further objections and praised God saying, "So then, God has even granted the Gentiles repentance unto life."' New Testament, New Covenant repentance is something granted by God. In the whole of the

Good News of the Gospel of Jesus Christ, the emphasis is upon what God has done for man. The Scriptures show that this is true in this fundamental matter of repentance.

In the Old Testament, Old Covenant repentance was something done by man to draw a response from God. In the New Testament, under the New Covenant, the order is reversed. In Romans 2:4 it says, 'Or do you show contempt for the riches of His [God's] kindness, tolerance and patience, not realising that God's **kindness leads you towards repentance**' (author's emphasis). Now the order is that God does something and man responds. It is God's kindness that leads a person to respond to God, and that response is called repentance. What was that kindness from God? It was that He gave His Son, Jesus Christ, for mankind - as it says in Ephesians 2:7, '. . . in the coming ages He [God] might show the incomparable riches of His grace, expressed in His kindness to us in Christ Jesus.' The Apostle Paul writes, in 2 Tim. 2:25, of how repentance is something granted by God. He writes, 'Those who oppose him [the Lord's servant] he must gently instruct in the hope that **God will grant them** repentance leading to a knowledge of the truth' (author's emphasis). The writer of the letter to the Hebrews brings out the point that '. . . repentance from acts that lead to death, . . .' is a foundation of the Christian Gospel. The question must be asked, 'What is it that, in a Gospel rooted in God's grace to man, will lead to death - and from which the Christian should, therefore, repent?' It is not the Christian's sins which lead to death - although that is how many would interpret that Scripture. It cannot be the Christian's sins because they are paid for, the Bible teaches, by the blood of Jesus. No, it is legalism which, under a Covenant of grace, leads to death. This is attested to in Hebrews 10:29, 'How much more severely do you think a man deserves to be punished who has trampled the Son of God under foot, who has treated as an unholy thing the blood of the covenant that sanctified him, and who has insulted the Spirit of grace.' It is legalism from which Christians are, in Hebrews 6:1, commanded to repent. A final Scripture worth quoting is in Hebrews 6:4,6 where the writer says, 'It is impossible for those who have once been enlightened ... if they fall away, to be brought back to repentance ...' So, contrary to the Old Covenant concept of repeated acts of repentance and, indeed, contrary to much modern teaching along the same lines, the Bible says that, under the New Covenant, it is impossible to repent a second time having once repented and then fallen away.

So, to summarize the major teachings on repentance under the New Covenant: it is a gift from Jesus, it is granted by God, it is man's response to God's kindness, it is a foundation of the Christian faith and it is impossible to return to it. That totally separates New Covenant repentance from Old Covenant repentance. The Christian must make sure that he or she is living under New Covenant repentance.

Jesus' teachings on repentance

When Jesus came He called upon people to repent and He taught about repentance. When Jesus sent out His disciples, He told them to go and preach that people should repent. Repentance is a major theme of the Gospel and in fact, as the writer to the Hebrews says, it is a foundation of the Christian faith. Unless there are major differences between what Jesus taught as repentance and what the Rabbis taught under the Old Covenant then, essentially, Jesus would have been only reinforcing Judaism. In His teachings Jesus gives His definition of repentance.

The Lost Sheep

In Luke 15 there are three separate stories all revolving around the issues of repentance. In the first story Jesus tells of some sheep, one of which becomes lost and ninety-nine which do not become lost. The shepherd searches for, and finds, the lost sheep. The shepherd then carries the lost sheep back home and, finally, invites his neighbours together to share his joy over the sheep being found. Jesus then says, in verse 7, 'I tell you that in the same way there will be more rejoicing in heaven over one sinner who repents than over ninety-nine righteous persons who do not need to repent.' Jesus draws a clear comparison between the one lost sheep and the one repentant sinner and between the ninety-nine sheep who did not get lost and the ninety-nine persons who did not need to repent.

Jesus says that the sequence of events which the lost sheep went through is 'in the same way' the path of a repentant sinner. In order, then, to understand Jesus' definition of repentance, the question must be asked, 'What did the lost sheep do that allows Jesus to liken it to a repentant sinner?' The Scriptures show that in the sequence of events in the opening story in Luke 15, the only active part played by the sheep was that it got lost. All other events affecting that sheep were initiated and carried through by the shepherd. The shepherd did the searching, the shepherd did the finding, the shepherd did the lifting and the carrying and, finally, the shepherd gathered his neighbours to share his joy. Throughout that sequence of events, Jesus says that lost sheep is like a repentant sinner.

The sheep contributes two things to the sequence of events which lead to it being restored to its home. Initially, the sheep gets lost; subsequently, the sheep accepts being found. It allows the shepherd to carry it home on his shoulders. Without the sheep's consent, the shepherd would not have been able to lift and carry a full-grown sheep. So the sheep got lost, and accepted being found. That, Jesus says, is repentance under the New Covenant. The Christian accepts that he is lost – that is why the Christian turned to Jesus and accepted Him as Lord and Saviour. New Covenant repentance requires one other thing – that the lost one should accept that he has been found and that it is the responsibility, and joy, of the Shepherd to carry him safe home, all the way to Glory.

There is no room in Jesus' story, and definition, for any concept of the repentant sinner contributing anything towards his salvation or his restoration. There is no suggestion of striving not to get lost again, no suggestion of contrition or sorrow, no suggestion of any burden or responsibility being placed upon, or accepted by, the repentant one at any point. How different from the Old Covenant where the burden was squarely upon the sinner to get right with God. Now it is God who makes man right with Himself. It should be noted that it is the shepherd's joy to carry the burden of the lost sheep until it is safe back home: '. . . he joyfully puts it on his shoulders and goes home.' It is Jesus' joy to carry the responsibility for not only the salvation of the lost sinner but, also, for the restoration of that lost sinner into the family of God and, eventually, right into Glory.

The Lost Coin
The story which follows, the Parable of The Lost Coin, illustrates the same points. It is the coin which is lost. The woman does the cleaning and the searching until the coin is found and restored. Again, Jesus likens that lost coin to a repentant sinner. So, again, the question must be asked, 'What does the coin do that allows Jesus to liken it to a repentant sinner?' As with the lost sheep, the answer to that question is that the coin became lost and then was found. The coin contributed nothing else to the sequence of events. The initiative and responsibility for locating and restoring the coin lay entirely with the woman. Just as with the Christian, the initiative and responsibility for his or her salvation and restoration lies entirely with God - accepting that truth is, according to the teachings of Christ, New Covenant repentance.

The problem for the Christian is not in accepting his lostness. Every Believer did that before accepting Jesus as Saviour - indeed, it is the recognizing of his need for a saviour that leads a Christian to accept the Saviour. The problem for the Christian is in accepting that he has been found and accepting that it is God's responsibility to restore him, both to the family of God and, eventually, into Glory. The Christian is tempted to believe that he or she has to make some contribution to the process, once they are found. In the face of such temptation the Christian should remember the lost sheep and the lost coin. A Christian can feel that their lifestyle is such that, after being saved, they are still a burden to Jesus. The Christian should remember, at such times, how Jesus taught of the joy with which the shepherd placed the sheep on his shoulders and carried it all the way home and then, still rejoicing, called together his neighbours to celebrate. The Christian should allow Jesus to be the burden-bearer - that is Christ's joy, to safeguard His flock right into Glory. Repentance as taught to the Jews required them to contribute to the process of

The Lost Son

The third story in Luke 15 is the well known Parable of The Lost Son – often referred to as the Parable of The Prodigal Son. This parable is dealt with in greater detail in another chapter; here it is sufficient to look at what it teaches about repentance. The son leaves home, squanders his inheritance, comes upon hard times, thinks of a way of saving himself and sets off back to his father's house. In verses 18-19 of this chapter the son is turning homeward and plans to say to his father, 'Father, I have sinned against heaven and against you. I am no longer worthy to be called your son; make me like one of your hired men.' Sadly, many Christians understand this as repentance. This 'turning back to the father' is actually taught as repentance. In fact, the young man is far from repentance at this point. He is going home with a plan which will allow him to be the author of his own salvation. He is to become like a hired man. In other words, he will work for his father and, that way, he will be able to pay back his father the money he has had and squandered. There is, at this point, no recognition by the son of his need for grace. There is, at this point, no understanding by the son that the father is bothered, not by the squandering of the money, but by the broken relationship between himself and his son.

So the son sets off home. The next sequence of events is initiated by the father. The son contributes nothing. The father sees the son coming, rushes out to meet him, throws his arms around the son and kisses him. This is not the welcome the son was expecting. The father asks no questions about the inheritance. He makes no demands for repayment. He awaits no expression of sorrow from the son. The father simply extends, unconditionally and very publicly, a father's love to his son. In verse 21 the son speaks to the father, and there is a marked difference between what he planned to say (in verse 19) and what he actually says. The son says, 'Father I have sinned against heaven and against you. I am no longer worthy to be called your son.' The son, in the face of overwhelming love, drops any idea of working for his father. He now understands that it is the broken relationship which is the issue between him and his father – it is not the squandered inheritance. He therefore, and quite rightly, confesses his unworthiness to sonship; but he then truly repents – that is, he accepts that he has been lost and has now been found – and accepts the freely offered gift of unconditional restoration to sonship. That acceptance is demonstrated in the subsequent verses in the passage.

The Greek word often used for repentance in the New Testament is metanoia, which means 'to change course after further insight.' The son in this story perfectly illustrates this. He came home with one course of action planned. He received further insight into the real issue through his father's demonstration of love. He then changed course, away from self-effort and towards total dependence upon an undeserved, and unconditional, free offer of salvation and restoration to sonship.

That is the same undeserved, unconditional, offer that God makes to each human being – restoration, through Jesus, into full sonship. Many Christians are still rooted in verse 19 – that is, recognizing their lostness but still relying on self-effort. They are, essentially, servants and not sons. The glory of understanding God's grace, and understanding repentance, is that it moves the Christians from verse 19 to verse 21 – from servanthood to sonship. The Christian, to determine his or her understanding of repentance, should ask of themselves the question, 'Am I in some way working for God (verse 19) as though I can pay Him back for the wrong I have done, or am I simply receiving from God (verse 21) what He is freely offering – even though I recognize I do not deserve such a gift?'

The sheep, the coin, the son – none of them did any of the things required under Old Testament, Old Covenant, repentance. Jesus teaches a new understanding of repentance. The Christian must make certain that he or she is living under New Testament, New Covenant repentance. The repentance Jesus teaches cannot happen without faith in Christ and, equally, there cannot be faith in Christ, as God's provision for the lost, without there being New Covenant repentance. So, in the New Covenant, faith and repentance become a single issue. Faith in God's offer of undeserved sonship brings an acceptance of, and dependence upon, that freely given offer. That is New Covenant faith and New Covenant repentance.

Why the difference between Old Covenant and New Covenant repentance?

The Old Covenant, that was instituted through Moses, was a covenant of Law, a covenant of works, a covenant of obedience. The New Covenant is a covenant of grace and faith. The focus has changed from what man had to do for God onto what God has done for man. In the Old Covenant God blessed His people as a result of obedience (Deut. 28); in the New Covenant, God blesses His people through His grace (John 1:16).

In the New Covenant the one issue between God and man is faith. In John 3:18, and elsewhere, the Scriptures make it clear that people will be condemned solely because they have not believed in God's Son. As, under the New Covenant – and according to the teachings of Christ Himself – faith and repentance are inseparable, any continuation of the Old Covenant concept of repentance is not only unnecessary but it is Scripturally impossible. Hence, the word for repentance is no longer 'to turn back' – that is, away from sin and back to the things of God; the word is now 'to change course after further insight.' That is, to change course from striving to keep right with God to having a saving faith that Jesus has made the Christian totally, and eternally, right with God.

Jesus' teachings demonstrated

When considering the following illustrations of Jesus' teachings on repentance, it is important to remember that forgiveness of sins, justification, or whatever other words are used to show a right relationship with God, cannot come without repentance. So if the New Testament Scriptures talk of sins being forgiven, or justification taking place, then repentance must also have taken place.

Matthew 21:28-32 The two sons

A man has two sons. He asks one to go and work in the vineyard and the son replies that he will not. Later he changes his mind and goes. The father asks the second son to work in the vineyard. The second son says he will go, but then he fails to do so, Which son, Jesus asked His listeners, did what the father wanted? The chief priests and the elders answered that the first son did the father's will. Many Christians would agree with that answer. If it is correct then Jesus is clearly teaching salvation by works and that it is only by doing what God asks that Christians carry out the Father's will. Old Covenant repentance was changing one's mind, or behaviour, and becoming obedient to God. That is what is illustrated by the first son. There is no grace in the relationship between the son and his father, the relationship is based upon works. With the second son, one can truly see the Christian. Here is a young man whose immediate response is to say 'Yes' to his father; but who subsequently fails to live out his initial intent. Is not that the position of every born again Believer? Does not the Christian's heart cry 'Yes' when he hear the Father's voice – and does not that Christian's sinful flesh often act as a barrier and so stop him fulfilling his heart's desire to serve God? The relationship between the second son and his father must depend upon grace; the relationship between the Christian and God must equally depend upon grace. Contrary to much modern teaching, it is the second son who does the father's will – albeit only in his initial heart response. The battle between the flesh and the spirit goes on; but the immediate response of the Christian to his Father's voice should never be, as it was with the first son, 'No, I will not do what you ask.' The Christian says 'Yes' and then fails. This story shows that New Covenant repentance is about heart intent not, as with Old Covenant repentance, a series of works and outward acts.

Mark 2:1-12 The paralytic

A paralytic is brought to Jesus. The friends of the paralytic are so determined to get their friend to Jesus that they lower him through the roof. The passage says, 'When Jesus saw their faith, He said to the paralytic, 'Son, your sins are forgiven.' Something which has already occurred in the passage constitutes repentance – because without repentance there can be no forgiveness of sins. What did the paralytic do that Jesus accepted as repentance? Jesus Himself answers that question. The Scriptures say He responded to their faith. The paralytic, and his friends, saw the hopelessness of his situation – accepted his lostness – and came to the only one who could do anything to change the situation. Faith in Jesus, that He can do for the Believer what he cannot do for himself, is under the New Covenant – as clearly illustrated in this story – repentance. There are no promises from the paralytic, there are no questions or conditions from Jesus; He simply saw the paralytic's faith, which demonstrated his repentance, and forgave him.

Luke 13:1-3 The murdered worshippers
In this short passage a group of Galileans are murdered by Roman soldiers whilst they are in the Temple offering sacrifices to God. Does not what Christians do for God demonstrate repentance? Apparently not, for Jesus warns the people to whom He is talking, 'Unless you repent you too will all perish.' Those who believe that a good life, with modern day 'sacrifices,' represent repentance are mistaken. Repentance is faith in God and His provision for us in Jesus. It is faith, not lifestyle, that counts in the New Covenant.

Luke 17:3-4 Self-effort or heart intent?
Jesus here instructs His followers that if anyone sins against them, even seven times a day (a term meaning many times, not literally limited to seven) and on each occasion says, 'I repent,' then the sinner is to be forgiven. Such a teaching suggests that repentance cannot involve any kind of effort on the part of man. Jesus teaches that if a man repeatedly sins each day it does not affect his entitlement to forgiveness if he says, 'I repent.' How many people would accept that another has repented when the sinning carried on unabated? Much modern teaching states that repentance involves a turning away from sin. Where is that in this teaching from Christ? Much modern teaching has Christians believing that repentance involves striving never to repeat a sin. Where is that in

'REPENT AND BELIEVE...'

this teaching? Both ideas are absent from the teachings of Christ because they represent Old Covenant repentance. However, with the understanding that New Covenant repentance means accepting one's lostness and accepting being found – that is, the receiving of the undeserved gift of forgiveness and reconciliation – then this teaching of Christ makes sense. It should be noted that this teaching relates to repentance and forgiveness between two people and, as such, should not be confused with the repentance and forgiveness which occurs between an individual and God.

Luke 18:9-14 The Pharisee and the tax collector
In this story told by Jesus, the Pharisee is very sure of his righteousness. It is based upon all that he has done – he is not a robber, an evildoer or an adulterer. He fasts and tithes. He gives thanks to God that he is such a man. The tax collector, though, will not even look up to pray. He simply confesses the hopelessness of his sinful self. Jesus teaches that it is the tax collector who goes home justified. As there can be no justification without repentance, what the tax collector did and/or said must constitute New Covenant repentance. What the tax collector did is entirely in keeping with the rest of Christ's teaching on repentance. The tax collector accepted his lostness and accepted that God was the only one who could change that situation. That is New Covenant repentance – to accept one's lostness and to receive mercy from the only One who can, through that mercy, change the situation.

Luke 18:18-29 The rich ruler
Here is a man who has made great efforts to keep right with God. He has kept the Commandments since he was a boy – yet still has no assurance of his salvation. Far from encouraging him, Jesus puts to the rich young ruler a demand which cultural expectations make it impossible to meet. The ruler goes away unhappy. He is still not right with God – and God has set him a standard which he simply cannot meet.

A rich man will give to the poor, will build synagogues, tithe his possessions and meet many requirements of the Law. The poor people hearing this thought (verse 26), 'If the rich, with all their opportunities to please God cannot get into heaven, then who can be saved?'

Jesus is pointing out to the people the utter hopelessness of their situation. He is pointing them to total dependence upon a Saviour. He is pointing them away from their lifestyle and towards a God of grace. He is calling them to repent.

Luke 23:42-43 The dying thief
The thief, dying on the cross alongside Jesus, offers Christ nothing but his faith. Jesus assures the thief that, on that very day, he will enter Paradise with Christ. If repentance is not an integral, and inseparable, part of faith then upon what basis did Jesus give His assurance to the thief – for without repentance there can be no forgiveness of sin? In these closing scenes of Jesus' crucifixion, He is demonstrating the principle of New Covenant repentance which He had repeatedly taught. That is that, under the New Covenant, the repentant sinner is one who comes empty-handed to God, recognizing his lostness, recognizing he can never change that lostness and ready to accept God's freely offered, unconditional salvation and restoration – to accept being found.

Summary
Repentance as something which man does as a contribution, in addition to faith, towards the gaining or keeping of his salvation has no Scriptural basis under the New Covenant. Repentance as something which man does for God is an Old Testament, Old Covenant concept – which has no place in the life of a Christian. Such a teaching makes repentance a burden, especially for the struggling Christian and, bringing no glory to Jesus, it should be strongly resisted.

Jesus teaches, and demonstrates, that faith and repentance are integral and inseparable parts of the same act. A person cannot repent without first having faith and, conversely, a person cannot have faith without repenting. The two go hand in hand. They are not separate issues. Jesus teaches, and demonstrates, that New Covenant repentance is the acceptance of being lost and, equally, the acceptance of being found – in other words the acceptance of God's freely offered grace. Repentance in the New Covenant has become total dependence upon God and what He has done for man.

'... and believe the Good News.'

The call of Jesus Christ was, and is, 'Repent, and believe the Good News.' The Good News which Jesus came to bring is both very comprehensive and yet, at the same time, very simple. There are many ways of expressing it. Here are some of the Scriptures which highlight some of the fundamental Good News which Jesus brought to man.

Salvation is:

A work of God for man. John 3:16 – 'For God so loved the world that He gave His one and only Son, that whoever believes in Him shall not perish but have eternal life.' God loves the world, God gave His Son. The Good News is that the Christian faith is about what God has done for man.

The gift of eternal life. Rom. 6:23 – 'For the wages of sin is death, but the gift of God is eternal life in Christ Jesus our Lord.' The Good News is that eternal life is a gift from God to man. A person does not work for, nor contribute towards, a gift. A gift is free. A gift carries no cost and no sense of obligation. Eternal life is a gift.

A God-given holiness. Eph. 1:4 – 'For He chose us in Him, before the creation of the world, to be holy and blameless in His sight...' The Good News is that God chose the Christian. God chose the Christian before time began. God chose to see the Christian as holy and blameless. All this is God working for man. The Christian's daily life does not have any bearing upon his standing before God. It is God's choice, not the Christian's effort – and that's Good News!

Divine reconciliation. 2 Cor. 5:19 – '... that God was reconciling the world to Himself in Christ, not counting men's sins against them.' The Good News is that God was doing the reconciling. God was bringing man back into a relationship with Himself and He was doing that through Christ. That reconciliation was made possible because God chose not to count men's sins against them. God was able to make that choice because Jesus Christ took those sins into Himself and died for them on Calvary's cross.

The cancelling of all sins. John 1:29 – 'The next day John [the Baptist] saw Jesus coming towards him and said, "Look, the Lamb of God who takes away the sin of the world."'

1 John 2:2 – 'He [Jesus] is the atoning sacrifice for our sins, and not only for ours but also for the sins of the whole world.' The Good News is that at Calvary's cross all sin was dealt with once and for all, as these two Scriptures testify. That is Good News for the Christian because it frees him or her from the fear that their daily life will somehow affect their salvation. Sin is not an issue now – it is only faith in Christ that God requires. This is Good News for the non-Christian. Jesus died for the sins of the whole world. Sin is not an issue between the unbeliever and God. God only requires faith. As all sin has been dealt with then the opportunity for reconciliation is available to all people.

Being acceptable to God. Rom. 15:16 – '[Paul] . . . a minister of Christ Jesus to the Gentiles with the priestly duty of proclaiming the gospel of God, so that the Gentiles might become an offering acceptable to God, sanctified by the Holy Spirit.' The Good News is that it is the Holy Spirit of Almighty God who sanctifies (sets apart, makes holy) the Believer. It is, once again, God working for man and not the other way around.

God loves man, gives him a free gift, chooses to see him as holy, does not count his sins against him and carries out the work of sanctification within man. That is, most definitely, very Good News!

Ephesians 2:8-9 'For it is by grace you have been saved, through faith – and this not of yourselves, it is the gift of God – not by works, so that no-one can boast.'

CHAPTER 7

The Commandments and the Christian

Introduction

The two Testaments of the Bible deal, essentially, with two covenants. One is the Covenant of Moses in the Old Testament and the other is the New Covenant of Christ in the New Testament. There are other covenants in the Old Testament. There is the Covenant with Abraham, which is directly linked to that of Christ. There is the covenant with Noah, which was a fairly restricted covenant, and the covenant with David. The major covenant, though, of the Old Testament is that of God with Moses.

There is a lot of confusion within Christianity as to where the Covenant of Moses fits in with the life of the Christian. What relationship is there between the Law of Moses - which includes the Ten Commandments - and the Christian? It is quite possible to live with a lot of spiritual confusion until this particular issue is understood. The norm for most Christians today, both in lifestyle and in teaching, is a mix of the Old and New Covenants - an irreconcilable mix of Law and grace, faith and works. It is quite common to end up with a blending of the old and new covenants. This is a blending that really isn't very comfortable to live with because, if it is really examined, it is full of contradictions and doesn't actually make any sense.

Colossians 1:6 says, 'All over the world this gospel is bearing fruit and growing, just as it has been doing among you *since* the day you heard it and understood God's grace in all its truth' (author's emphasis). This Scripture, and many others, underlines the vital importance of understanding, and separating, the two major covenants - that of Law and works from that of grace and faith. The Bible says that only when God's grace is truly understood does the Gospel really grow and bear fruit. This chapter will seek to separate Moses from Christ, Law from grace.

Separating the Covenants

It is very important to understand under which covenant Christians are living because it is not at all uncommon to hear Moses being applied to Christians. Some of the differences are set out in the table below:

MOSES		CHRIST	
Law	Exod. 24:12	Grace	Titus 3:7
Works	Deut. 6:25	Faith	Eph. 2:8
Israel only	Rom. 2:14	For all mankind	John 3:16
Conditional blessings	Deut. 28:1-2	Unconditional blessings	John 1:16
Limited in time	Gal. 3:19	Eternal	Heb. 13:20
Gave no righteousness	Rom. 9:31	Given righteousness	Rom. 5:17
Held man prisoner	Gal. 3:23	Set man free	Heb. 9:15
Lower standard	Matt. 5:21	Higher standard	Matt. 5:22
A shadow of reality	Heb. 10:1	Reality	Col. 2:17
A distant relationship	Exod. 19:24	Intimacy	Rom. 8:15
		Unaffected by Moses	Gal. 3:17

The differences explained

Law – not grace

The Covenant of Moses is the Law of Moses which includes the Ten Commandments. Christians, when talking of the Law of Moses, tend very much to focus on the Ten Commandments but, in fact, it includes hundreds of other commandments covering every aspect of personal, social, religious and national life.

The Covenant of Christ is, on the other hand, a covenant of grace. The Christian's relationship with God does not depend upon countless rules and regulations, it does not depend upon the Christian doing something for God but, instead, depends upon God doing something for mankind. Titus 3:7 says, '... having been justified by His grace, we might become heirs having the hope of eternal life.' Christians are made right with God through His grace. That is the fundamental truth, and Good News, of the New Covenant. The Christian's relationship with God has nothing to do with his own effort. Under the Covenant of Moses a Law was given and had to be obeyed. A relationship with God was only possible through obedience and the blessings received also depended upon obedience. Neither of those applies in Christ – the relationship and the blessings are through grace, and grace alone.

Works – not faith

The Covenant of Moses is a covenant of works under which God called Israel into a relationship with Himself based very strictly on their obedience. Moses says in Deuteronomy 28:1, 'If you fully obey the Lord your God and carefully follow all His commands that I give you today, the Lord your God will set you high above all the nations on earth. All these blessings will come upon you and accompany you, if you obey the Lord your God...' There then follows eleven verses outlining how God is going to highly bless Israel, if they obey Him. The other side of the coin is that if Israel is disobedient, in that same chapter – Deuteronomy 28, Moses says, 'However, if you do not obey the Lord your God and do not carefully follow all His commands and decrees I am giving you today, all these curses will come upon you and overtake you...' There are then 53 verses of how God is going to curse Israel, and punish Israel, if they do not obey Him. Fifty-three verses where God says, 'I will curse you in the fields and I will curse you in the cities, I will curse you in your womb. I will curse you in your crops. I will hand you over to you enemies.' Every area of life will be cursed by God if Israel does not obey Him.

These are not idle threats. Daniel testifies in Daniel 9:11, when he prays from exile after Israel has been swept aside by her enemies, 'All Israel has transgressed Your Law, and turned away, refusing to obey You. Therefore the curses and sworn judgments written in the Law of Moses, the servant of God, have been poured out on us, because we have sinned against You.' So what God said, God meant! 'If you do not obey Me, I will curse you.'

In Christ, it is a covenant of faith – 'For it is by grace you have been saved, through faith – and this is not from yourselves, it is the gift of God' (Eph. 2:8). Even the faith by which Christians are saved is, the Bible says, a gift from God.

These first two revelations about the Covenant of Moses show very much that the emphasis is upon man, whereas in Christ the emphasis is not upon what man is doing for God but upon what God has done for man.

National – not universal

The Law of Moses was given to Israel, and Israel alone. The writer of Psalm 147 says, 'He [God] has revealed His Word to Jacob, His laws and decrees to Israel. He has done this for no other nation; they do not know His laws.' Paul refers to this truth in Romans 2:14 when he is speaking of the Gentiles. He writes, 'Indeed when Gentiles who do not have the law...' That phrase makes it perfectly clear that the Law was not given to the Gentiles. In Romans 9:4 Paul is writing about Israel. He says, '...the people of Israel. Theirs is the adoption as sons; theirs the divine glory, the covenants, the receiving of the law...' The Law was never given to the Gentiles. There is not one single verse in the whole of Scripture to show that the Law, including the Ten Commandments, was ever given, or extended, to the Gentiles. It was given to Israel, it remained with Israel. It is an error that the Ten Commandments have become such a central pillar of the Christian church when they were never once given to the Christians. The Christian Church has taken on something to which it has no right. In Galatians 3:15 Paul writes that no-one can add or take away from a duly established covenant. God established the Covenant of Moses, consisting of the Law of Moses with its Ten Commandments, with Israel. No-one can add in the Gentiles simply because it seems a good code of moral living – nor, indeed, for any other reason. The Covenant of Moses was never given to the Gentiles. It was given for a specific purpose, in that Moses said, 'If you fully obey the Lord your God and carefully follow all His commands that I give you today, the Lord your God will set you high above all the nations on earth' (Deut. 28:1). That was God's purpose – that Israel should be an example to the nations of the world. This is such an important point because those who argue in favour of adherence to the Ten Commandments as Christian guidance have no Biblical mandate and, in fact, are teaching and acting contrary to the Word of God. On the other hand, the Covenant of Christ was offered to the whole world – to Jew and Gentile alike. 'For God so loved the world that He gave His one and only Son that *whoever* believes in Him shall not perish but have eternal life' (John 3:16, author's emphasis). Now the whole world is offered reconciliation with God, now the whole world is offered salvation. There is no need to try and add the Gentiles to the Covenant of Moses; now there is a Covenant for the Gentiles, as well as the Jews. It is a Covenant for which there is a Biblical mandate; it is the Covenant of Christ.

Conditional blessings – not unconditional
In Deut. 28:2 Moses says to Israel, 'All these blessings will come upon you and accompany you if you obey the Lord your God . . .' Blessings followed obedience under the Covenant of Moses. If there was no obedience then not only was Israel not blessed, she was actually cursed and punished by God – as Deut. 28 goes on to make clear. Under the Covenant of Christ, the Christian receives, 'From the fullness of His grace . . . one blessing after another' (John 1:16). Now the blessings are dependent not upon man's efforts and man's obedience; they are dependent solely upon God's grace.

Limited in time – not eternal
The Covenant of Moses was limited in time. It has a beginning and it has a Biblically declared end. In Galatians 3:19 Paul, writing about the Law, says, 'It was added because of transgressions *until* the Seed to whom the promise referred had come' (author's emphasis). In Galatians 3:16 Paul has already explained that 'the Seed' referred to is Jesus Christ. So the Law was given to Moses and was to apply until the coming of Christ – or, more specifically, until the death of Christ. From the moment the Law of Moses, with its Ten Commandments, was given it had an end point. That end point was Calvary's cross because it was there that the Law was fulfilled, abolished and cancelled. (Eph. 2:15; Col. 2:14). How can it be that 2,000 years after its fulfillment, abolition and cancellation Christians are still applying aspects of the Law of Moses to their life and relationship with God? It can only be because there is a woeful lack of understanding of the Scriptures and of the basic truths of the glorious Gospel of Christ. On the other hand, the Gospel of Christ is eternal. Hebrews 13:20, as one example of

many, says as much, 'May the God of peace who, through the blood of the eternal covenant brought back from the dead our Lord Jesus . . .' Another clear contrast with the covenant of Moses.

Unrighteousness – not righteousness

The Law of Moses cannot, and was never intended to, give righteousness. Romans 9:31-32 says, '. . . Israel, who pursued a law of righteousness has not attained it. Why not? Because they pursued it not by faith but as if it were by works.' Even though Paul could write about himself that, '. . . as for legalistic righteousness, faultless' (Phil. 3:6), yet he came to realize that he still fell so far short of the glory of God that he needed a Saviour. The Law of Moses was never intended to give righteousness. Indeed, as Paul writes in Galatians 2:21, '. . . if righteousness could be gained through the law, Christ died for nothing.'

On the other hand, under the Covenant of Christ, Christians are given righteousness as a gift. Rom. 5:17 speaks of how those '. . . who receive God's abundant provision of grace and of the gift of righteousness [will] reign in life through the one man, Jesus Christ.' Righteousness, which could never be earned under the Old Covenant, is now a gift under the New Covenant. The Old Covenant, that of Moses, had Israel struggling to achieve righteousness and utterly failing; the New Covenant leaves the Christian in receipt of the free gift of righteousness. The free gift of right standing before God. There are those who would still teach that a Christian has to contribute something towards how he or she stands before God. That is where so much of the struggling and disillusionment comes from in the life of a Christian – a sense of having failed God and, having fallen so short of His desired standard, become unacceptable to God. Yet the Good News of the Gospel of Christ is that a Christian cannot fall short of God's required standard because that standard is met only by Christ and the benefits of Christ's work are then freely given to the Believer.

Imprisonment – not freedom

Those who argue in favour of Christians adhering to the Ten Commandments, or any other aspects of the Covenant of Moses, ignore Scriptures such as Galatians 3:23 which states that, 'Before this faith came, we were held prisoners by the law, locked up until faith should be revealed.' The Law held its followers as prisoners! Who would sensibly argue in favour of being held a prisoner? The limit upon this imprisonment, this Law, is actually set out in this same verse of Scripture: '. . . we were held prisoners by the law, locked up *until* faith should be revealed' (author's emphasis). The Law is not portrayed as the friend of the Christian, nor is it put forward as the rule of life for the Christian. It is important to remember that any talk of the Law includes the Ten Commandments; because it is that part of the Law which is so revered by the Christian Church - and even taught by the Church and applied to Christians today. It is almost deemed heretical to suggest the Ten Commandments have no relevance whatsoever to the Christian - and it is this attitude that allows the Law, and legalism, to still have a hold over Christians. To be held a prisoner is, obviously, not a good or comfortable position in which to be. It is this wrong application of the Law to Christians that brings the lack of comfort so many Christians experience - even to the point of falling completely away from any fellowship with fellow Believers.

On the other hand, as the Law held its followers prisoner, so Jesus Christ sets Believers free. Gal. 5:1 says, 'It is for freedom that Christ has set us free.' If it was for freedom that Christ came, then from what did man need to be set free? Galatians 3:23 says it was the Law, holding man prisoner, from which he needed to be set free. Christ has now set Believers free from the Law; faith has been revealed. All Christians should follow the instruction of Gal 5:1 and, 'Stand firm, then, and do not let yourselves be burdened again by a yoke of slavery.'

Second best – not the best

Some would argue that, 'The Commandments are a good rule of life, anyway, and it doesn't do any harm to try and live by them.' Firstly, there is no Divine mandate for the Christian to try and live according to the Ten Commandments; so it does do harm in the sense that it puts that person outside of the will of God. Secondly Matthew 5:21 compared with Matthew 5:22 shows the contrast for those who would uphold the Ten Commandments. In the two verses mentioned Jesus says (Matt. 5:21), 'You have heard that it was said to the people long ago, do not murder and anyone who murders will be subject to judgement.' All God required from those who lived according to the Ten Commandments was that they did not murder someone else. Jesus Christ, however, sets a much higher standard. Jesus goes on (Matt. 5:22), 'But I tell you, that anyone who is angry with his brother will be subject to judgement.' Those who argue in favour of the Ten Commandments are arguing for a lower standard of living than Christ demands of His people. Christ can make that demand because He gives Believers the Holy Spirit to outwork that demand. He doesn't expect anything from His followers that He does not first equip them for. No-one should argue that the Ten Commandments are a 'good rule for life.' It isn't good enough any more simply not to kill people. As a result of the revelation of Christ's love, and the gift of the Holy Spirit, now the Christian is required not even to be angry with people. This higher standard applies to every area of a Christian's life. It brings no glory to Christ to argue in favour of something that is second best.

Shadow – not reality
In Hebrews 10:1 it is written 'The law is only a shadow of the good things that are coming - not the realities themselves.' In Colossians 2:17 it tells where those realities are to be found. There it is written, 'These [the things of the Law] are a shadow of the things that were to come; the reality, however, is found in Christ.' Christians should not argue in favour of a shadow; let Christians argue for reality – Christ, and all that He is and all that He has achieved.

Distant relationship – not intimacy
A distant relationship was all that could be expected under the Law of Moses. The distant relationship was declared, by God, with

the giving of the Law. God instructed Moses 'Go down and bring Aaron up with you. But the priests and the people must not force their way through to come up to the Lord, or He will break out against them' (Exod. 19:24). This distant relationship continued throughout the days of the Old Covenant. The High Priest was the only one who could minister before God. When he did it was necessary to wear bells on his priestly robes. The purpose of the bells was to enable God to hear them so that the High Priest would not die as he entered and left the Holy Place.

On the other hand, in Christ, Christians are given a spirit that cries, 'Abba, Father' (Rom. 8:15). Christians are offered not distance, but intimacy; not servanthood, but sonship. Unless Christians understand the differences between these two Covenants and can separate them and live under the one which is appropriate to them, there will always be confusion in the Christian's relationship with God. One minute the freedom of Christ, the next the imprisonment of the Law. One minute intimacy and love, the next distance and fear. Christians in such a position have very little Good News to share - it is so blurred by the bad news that their ability to witness is greatly reduced. Christians have a wonderful message to share; but Believers must be able to separate themselves from a covenant which, in reality, has never applied to them.

A Biblical confirmation

The Bible specifically teaches that the grace Covenant under which the Christian lives is not in any way affected by the Covenant of Moses - which, it must be stated again, includes the Ten Commandments. In Galatians 3 Paul has been contrasting the Law and the Covenant of the Promise. In verse 17 he writes, 'What I mean is this: The law, introduced 430 years later, [that is, after the Covenant of Abraham] does not set aside the covenant previously established by God and thus do away with the promise.' The original Covenant was with Abraham. Abraham believed God and it was credited to him as righteousness - it was a covenant of faith between God and Abraham (Gen. 15:6). Paul writes, in Gal. 3:16, that, 'The promises were spoken to Abraham and to his seed.' Paul explains that the Bible 'does not say 'and to seeds' meaning many people, but, 'and to your seed' meaning one person' who is Christ.' Paul is making it clear that the heir of Abraham is not Israel, but Jesus Christ – one man. Galatians 3 explains a very important doctrinal point. The Covenant of faith was with Abraham, long before the Law was given. A Covenant cannot be added to or taken away from. Christ is the heir of the Abrahamic Covenant and Christians are heirs with Him. Accordingly, the Law has no relevance to the Christian as he is under another Covenant. Gal. 3:29 says, 'If you belong to Christ, then you are Abraham's seed and heirs according to the promise.'

So there is the Biblical confirmation that the Christian is utterly unaffected by the Law of Moses and should not be living under it, applying it to his relationship with God nor teaching it to others as a relevant rule of life or moral code. It is a witness of how far this legalism has taken over from faith that most non-Christians, and a large number of Christians, see Christianity as a set of 'Do's' and 'Don'ts.'

Christ's two Covenant ministry

What is rarely taught about Jesus Christ is that He had a two Covenant ministry. He was, as Simeon declared in Luke 2:32, both, '. . . a light for revelation to the Gentiles and for glory to Your people Israel.' Jesus Christ was the long awaited Prophet for Israel, but He was also the one to bring salvation to the Gentiles. Jesus came to end one Covenant, and then, to start a New Covenant. Failure to recognize this two Covenant ministry leads to utter confusion when looking at the teachings of Christ. When speaking to Israel, Jesus spoke as someone living under the Law of Moses. He had to do this because Israel, and Jesus as an Israelite, was under the Law of Moses and, as Jesus said in Matt. 5:18, the Law would remain in place, '. . . until everything is accomplished.' That is why Jesus, when answering the lawyer in Luke 10, pointed out obedience to the Law as the way to inherit eternal life (Luke 10:25-28). When speaking, though, in His role as Messiah of the world Jesus spoke as the initiator of the New Covenant. Thus, in John 6:28-29, when others come and ask, 'What must we do to do the works God requires?' Jesus does not point them to the Law but, rather, to Himself when He replies, 'The work of God is this: to believe in the One He has sent.'

Those two teachings of Jesus are irreconcilable. In one Jesus says that obedience to the Law of Moses is the way to be right with God, in the other Jesus says that faith in Him is the way to get right with God. There are many such instances in the teachings of Christ, where one teaching appears to contradict another. In reality, they actually do contradict each other, because the two Covenants contradict each other. Grace not Law, faith not works, eternal not limited and so on. In another sense, though, the teachings of Jesus are never contradictory; it is simply that the New Covenant is replacing the Old. That replacement did not fully take place until, at Calvary's cross, '... everything is accomplished.' Hence the need for the dual approach adopted by Jesus – one for the Jews and one for the whole world, including the Jews.

Jesus, as a Jew born under the Law, living under the Law could not speak against the Law – it was the God-given rule of life for the Jew. Jesus, as the Son of God and Saviour of both Jew and Gentile could not uphold the Law, but must rather uphold grace. Unless Christians are aware of, and accept, this two Covenant ministry they will be left with countless Scriptures which are impossible to reconcile. Christians will be, and often are, left very confused about the message that Jesus came to bring.

An important question to ask whenever reading the teachings of Jesus is, 'Who was He speaking to? In what role was He giving this teaching?' Without such questioning there is no separation of Jesus' teachings as One living under the Law and the One who had come to be the fulfillment of the Law – the One who came to abolish the Law (Eph. 2:15, Col. 2:14). An understanding of this two Covenant ministry removes any confusion from what Jesus taught. It becomes apparent that, when speaking as Messiah of the world, Jesus excluded the Law from all of His teaching.

The Apostle Paul's move from Moses to Christ

Paul – The Jew
Paul, before his conversion, was a zealous follower of the Law of Moses. He writes of himself, in Philippians 3:4-6, '. . . Circumcised on the eighth day, of the people of Israel, of the tribe of Benjamin, a Hebrew of Hebrews; in regard to the law, a Pharisee; as for zeal, persecuting the church; as for legalistic righteousness, faultless.'

Paul – The Christian
How dramatically Paul turned his back on that sort of position can be seen from his writing in 1 Cor. 9:20-22. The man who had described himself as 'a Hebrew of Hebrews' now writes, 'To the Jews I became as a Jew . . .' As a Christian, *Paul no longer thinks of himself as a Jew*. He no longer lives as a Jew. As someone who no longer saw himself as a Jew, Paul was no longer bound by the Law because that only applied to the Jews. Much of Paul's troubles, reflected in his writings, came because he was so often accused of setting aside the Law of Moses and teaching others to do the same. Here Paul writes that he reverted to his Jewish position only to win fellow Jews to Christ.

Paul then makes very clear his position, and therefore every Christian's position, in regard to the Law. He writes, 'To those under the law I became like one under the law (*though I myself am not under the law*)' . . . (author's emphasis). Paul boldly proclaims that he is not under Law. Christians who seek to, or teach others to, live under the Law – even if it is only the Ten Commandments as a rule of life – are taking a position contrary to the life and teachings of the Apostle Paul. If the Law did not apply to Paul it cannot apply to any Christian.

In his next utterance Paul begins to reveal the answer to those who say that to fully embrace grace will lead to licence. Paul writes, 'To those not having the law [that is the Gentiles] I became like one not having the law (though *I am not free from God's law but am under Christ's law*)' (author's emphasis). This is the first reference in the New Testament to the law which, with the change of priesthood from Aaron to Christ, replaced the Law of

Moses. It is the first reference to the rule of life which now applies to the Christian Believer. Paul has earlier stated that he is not 'under *the* Law' which is the title always given to the Law of Moses; but he now clarifies his position and states that he is not free from God's law. It is the change of law referred to in Hebrews 7:12; it is not lawlessness, nor licence. This is a very reassuring Scripture for those who fear that living fully under grace will lead to licence. It won't; but living fully under grace does mean living under Christ's law not the Law of Moses. Finally, it is worth noting that Paul finishes this passage by saying that, 'To the weak, I became weak . . .' Living under Christ's law, living under grace, was a source of strength to Paul and he only left that position and 'became weak' in order 'to win the weak.' Jesus Christ is the source of strength in the life of a Christian and part of Christ's provision, which makes Christians strong, is His law.

'What then is the purpose of The Law?'

If the Law of Moses, including the Ten Commandments, is so irrelevant to the Christian then the question must arise, 'What, then, was the purpose of the Law?' That is the very question Paul addresses in Gal. 3:19.

The Law makes man aware of his sin. Having asked the question in exactly those words, Paul then, in the same verse, gives the answer: 'It was added because of transgressions until the Seed to whom the promise referred had come.' Through Adam all mankind inherited the sin nature. What each individual must do is accept personal responsibility for his sinful actions. The Law achieves this. Paul writes, in Rom. 7:7, 'Indeed I would not have known what sin was except through the law. For I would not have known what coveting really was if the law had not said, 'Do not covet.'' The Law reveals to individuals their sinfulness, that is one of its purposes. It must be remembered that the overriding purpose of God is to reveal His grace in bringing salvation through Jesus Christ (Eph. 2:6-7). The purpose of man knowing his sinfulness is, quite simply, that he may come to know his need for a Saviour. So it makes great sense for God to reveal His standard to mankind even though He knows that man is incapable of meeting that standard. The only person likely to receive a Saviour is one who knows his need of a Saviour.

The Law highlights a man's lostness. The Law, the Bible teaches, reveals the sinfulness of sin. Rom. 7:13, speaking of the Law, says, 'Did that which is good, then, become death to me? By no means! But in order that sin might be recognized as sin, it produced death in me through what was good, so that through the commandment sin might become utterly sinful.' It is not enough for a person to know that he is a sinner. Each person needs to know that he or she is steeped in sin. Each one has to see the hopelessness of his position - that to sin is an integral part of the fallen human nature.

The Law leads a sinner to Christ. Galatians 3:24 says, 'So the law was put in charge to lead us to Christ, that we might be justified by faith.' The Law, through revealing a person's hopeless position before God, will lead that person to Christ as his Saviour. Whether Jew or Gentile, the mercy of God is that He allows the Law of Moses to lead even Gentiles, to whom it does not apply, to Christ. Once a person understands his need for a Saviour, and turns to Christ, then the Law has fulfilled its purpose. Gal. 3:24 goes on to say, 'Now that faith has come, we are no longer under the supervision of the law.' Paul is writing to Jewish Believers but it equally applies to Christian Believers who have erroneously put themselves under the Law, and the Ten Commandments.

The Law – a curse, a condemnation, death. One thing is certain, the Law was never given as a rule of life for the Christian. It is an indication of the confusion which exists within the Christian church that in hundreds of churches around this country can be seen, in stained glass windows, on plaques and in other ways, a Jewish Covenant displayed as something worthy of adherence. Yet The Bible says the Law, which was good, became (i) *A curse* - Gal. 3:10, 'All who rely on observing the law are under a curse, for it is written, "Cursed is everyone who does not continue to do EVERYTHING written in the Book of the Law"' (author's emphasis) - that is worth pondering when it is remembered that the Law is far more than the Ten Commandments, it is hundreds of rules and regulations; (ii) The Law became *a condemnation* – 2 Cor. 3:9, 'If the ministry that condemns men [verse 7 – 'engraved in letters of stone'] is glorious, how much more glorious is the ministry that brings righteousness!' (iii) The Law became ***death*** – Rom. 7:10, 'I found that the very commandment that was intended to bring life actually brought death.'

When Christians study the Scriptures, on the subject of the Law, it quickly becomes apparent that the Law, including the Ten Commandments, never did apply to the Gentiles and certainly doesn't apply to born-again Believers today.

Some New Testament Scriptures on the Law

Understanding what the New Testament teaches about the Law will stop the tendency which exists today – and in the time of Jesus and the Apostle Paul – of placing Believers under the Law. This is a look at just a few of the many New Testament Scriptures which deal with the Law and its relationship to the Believer.

Love – not legalism. Matt. 12:1-8. In this passage Jesus and His disciples are walking through a corn field on a Sabbath and His disciples begin to pick some of the corn to eat. The Pharisees immediately question Jesus about why He is allowing His disciples to break the Law. Jesus' answer incorporates the statement, 'If you had known what these words mean, 'I desire mercy, not sacrifice,' you would not have condemned the innocent.' Jesus is clearly already pointing the Pharisees beyond the legalism of Moses and towards the Law of Love. If the Law of Moses still applies then today Christians are left with the same question asked by the Pharisees. The actions of the disciples in this passage were an undoubted breaking of the fourth Commandment. Jesus is showing that, in Him – as the Scriptures elsewhere state – the Law is fulfilled and abolished

Believers not under the Law. Acts 15:5-11. The debate about the role of the Law of Moses in the grace dispensation goes right back to the early church in Jerusalem. In this passage this issue comes to head and a common position is agreed by the apostles. Some Believers had been teaching new Believers that unless they were circumcised, that is, they put themselves under the authority of the Law, they could not be saved. In the very arising of the question there is a demonstration that the Law did not apply to the Gentiles, which is why these Gentile Believers are being told they must *now* 'be circumcised and required to obey the law of Moses.' After much discussion amongst the apostles and elders, Peter addresses the early Believers. In his address he asks the question, of those who would apply the Law to the new Believers, 'Now then, why do you try to test God by putting on the necks of the disciples a yoke that neither we nor our fathers have been able to bear? No! We believe it is through the grace of our Lord Jesus that we are saved, just as they are.' Anyone, today, seeking to put a Believer under the Law, usually in the form of the Ten Commandments, should be asked the same question, 'Why are you doing that?'

No Law – no sin. Rom. 7:8. This Scripture gives a very strong and clear reason why Christians should resist any attempt to put them under the Law. This verse says, in part, 'For apart from law, sin is dead.' That is part of the glorious Good News of the New Covenant. Anyone struggling today with sin does not have to strive, does not have to make a superhuman effort to rid themselves of that sin. Such a struggling Believer simply has to come out from under law and live in grace. Rom. 5:17 says that 'those who receive God's abundant provision of grace and of the gift of righteousness [will] reign in life through the one man, Jesus Christ.' What hope, what peace, what joy can be offered to the struggling Christian when he is pointed not to himself but to the cross of Christ. Rom. 4:15 makes the same point that, 'And where there is no law there is no transgression.' In 1 John 3:4 it says, 'Everyone who sins breaks the law...' Clearly, if the Law is removed, so is sin. And that is the achievement of Christ on Calvary's cross. The Law was removed and so was sin. Many Christians still believe that sin is an issue between the Believer and God; but where is Christ in such an understanding? No! The Good News is that the Law, and sin, have been dealt with by Jesus.

The Law gives sin its power. 1 Cor. 15:56. This is another Scripture which makes plain the foolishness of those who advocate the Ten Commandments as a good rule of life. For those struggling with sin it is encouraging to know that it is the Law which gives sin its power – for that is what this Scripture says. Anyone battling to overcome sin should, therefore, set aside the legalism which so defeats and demoralises and should live in the grace which God extends to man through Jesus. The power the Law has is not that to actually make a person repeat that same old habit or thought pattern; but the power to bring guilt, failure and even condemnation. The power to make the Christian draw back from fellowship with God and with fellow Believers. Just as the Law, when originally given to Moses, initiated a distant relationship with the Lord, so the Law today brings that same distancing. The Law has power to isolate and weaken even further. That is the power the Law gives to sin. Accordingly any attempt to impose the Law (the Commandments) on a Believer should be resisted.

The Law abolished. Eph. 2:14-15. This Scripture clearly states that Jesus Christ abolished the Law. All major translations of the Bible use the word 'abolished' or 'abolishing' with regard to what Christ has done to the Law. So even those who find it difficult to accept that the Ten Commandments (and the rest of the Law) never applied to the Christian must, surely, accept that the Law no longer applies. Christian should always point others to Jesus and His achievement; not to an obsolete 'Jewish Law' – as the *Good News* translation refers to it. Col. 2:14 also speaks of God '... having cancelled the written code ...' There are those who argue that this refers only to the ceremonial law – but Col. 2:16 makes specific reference to the fourth Commandment, the keeping of the Sabbath.

The Law has changed. Heb. 7:12. This verse says, 'For when there is a change of the priesthood, there must also be a change of the law.' Christian Believers are not under the priesthood of Aaron. Hebrews 4:14 says that Christians have a new High Priest – Jesus Christ. As the priesthood has changed, so the law has changed – that is the Word of God. Not the priesthood of Aaron and the Law of Moses; but the High Priesthood of Christ and 'the law of Christ' (1 Cor. 9:21).

Obey all the Law – or none. James 2:10. For reasons which are hard to understand, apart from lack of knowledge of the Scriptures, the Christian Church has made a 'sacred cow' out of the

Ten Commandments and chosen to totally ignore the rest of the Law of Moses. Yet James writes here that if anyone seeks to keep the Law then such a person must keep ALL of the Law. If a person breaks one point of the Law, James says, then that person has effectively broken all the Law. Some may argue that only the Ten Commandments were given directly by God and the others were added on by man; but, the early books of the Bible are full of rules and regulations – they are in Scripture and 2 Timothy 3:16 says that, 'All Scripture is God-breathed . . .' So Christians cannot ignore hundreds of Scriptural rules and commands and simply seek to hold on to the Ten commandments; there is no integrity in such a position or such a teaching.

Other New Testament teaching on the Law

The Law is for those under law. Rom. 3:19. The Law was never given to the Gentiles, so it does not apply to Gentiles.

The Law only makes us conscious of sin. Rom. 3:20. The sin of the Christian has been dealt with in Christ. The Law, therefore, has no purpose in the life of a Christian (Rom. 5:20; Rom. 8:3; Gal. 3:21).

Justified by faith – not by observing the Law. Rom. 3:28; Gal. 3:11.

The Law invalidates faith. Rom. 4:14.

The Law brings wrath. Rom. 4:15.

The Law gives sin its mastery in a person's life. Rom. 6:14.

Believers are dead to the Law. Rom. 7:4.

The Law arouses sinful passions. Rom. 7:5. Hence Rom. 6:14; 1 Cor. 15:56 etc.

Free from the Law. Rom 7:6. Even those who were under the Law have now been set free from it.

Christ is the end of the Law. Rom. 10:4. A very simple statement.

Redeemed from the curse of the Law. Gal. 3:13. Failure to keep all the Law brings a curse. Christ bore that curse in Himself.

Set free from slavery. Gal. 5:1. Man was a slave to sin; held prisoner by the Law. Christ has set the Believer free from both.

Christians not under Law. Gal. 5:18. Having been born of the Spirit (John 3:6), every born-again Believer is led by the Spirit and, therefore, not under Law.

The Law is for the unrighteous. 1 Tim 1:9. The Good News is that God in Jesus has made the Christian righteous. 2 Cor. 5:21 says, 'God made Him who had no sin to be sin for us, so that in Him we might become the righteousness of God.' If the Law is for the unrighteous and the Christian, in Christ, is righteous then the Law, including the Ten Commandments, is not for the Christian.

The Commandments of Christ

One of the objections of those who oppose grace in all its fullness is the fact that Jesus gave commandments and, they argue, these HAVE to be obeyed – even if the Law of Moses doesn't.

Jesus did, indeed, give many commandments to His followers; however, Jesus did not use the phrase, 'My commandment' until the last supper. The reason for this is that at the last supper the whole of His talk to the disciples is set after the cross. That whole section of Scripture, John 13 to John 17, is Jesus speaking as the Saviour of the world. He is speaking as One who has brought to an end the rule of the Law of Moses – were the Law still applicable He would have had neither need, nor right, to impose new commandments. All the commandments, therefore, of Christ are given within the grace dispensation. In the passage of Scripture John 13 to John 17 there is only one reference to the Law of Moses. It is in John 15:25. Speaking of the events that are to unfold after the last supper, Jesus says, 'But this is to fulfil what is written in *their* Law:"They hated Me without reason"' (author's emphasis). In this one reference to the Law of Moses Jesus is clearly disassociating Himself and, thereby, His followers from the Law of the Jews.

The commandments given by Christ form what Paul refers to as 'Christ's law' (1 Cor. 9:21). They are to be obeyed; however, it must be remembered that they are given, and only take effect, within the Covenant of grace. These commandments given by Jesus represent the only Biblical 'Rule of Life' for the Christian. Any other rule of life, including adherence to the Ten Commandments, is self-imposed and has no biblical mandate or Divine authority behind it. The nature of Christ's commandments make clear that they do, indeed, come under the New Covenant. The New Covenant, the new law, is a Covenant and law of grace and love. Many of Christ's teachings and actions demonstrate the supremacy of love over legalism. It was this issue that brought Him into such direct conflict with the Pharisees and teachers of the Law. Christ's commandments reflect this supremacy of love. In His teaching at the last supper, Jesus instructs His followers, 'A new command I give you: love one another. As I have loved you, so you must love one another.' In John 15:12 Jesus says, 'My command is this: Love each other as I have loved you.' Again in John 15:17 Jesus says, 'This is My command: Love each other.' In 2 John verse 6 the apostle writes, 'As you have heard from the beginning, His command is that you walk in love.' The Apostle Paul sums up the commands of Christ when writing to the Galatians. In his letter Paul writes, Gal. 6:2, 'Carry each other's burdens, and in this way you will fulfil the law of Christ.'

So there are commandments for the Christian to obey. Setting aside the Law of Moses does not leave the Christian living a lawless, licentious life. The commands given by Christ, though, are set within the grace Covenant – so whether or not the Christian obeys them will not affect his standing before God. Ignoring the commands of Christ will have a detrimental effect upon the Christian witness and upon the well-being of his fellow man – and that is the motivation for keeping Christ's commands. It is not fear of punishment, not fear of being loved and blessed less by God – it is love of fellow man that motivates a Christian to live as Christ commands. This is the hallmark of the Christian, as Christ Himself said in John 13:35, 'All men will know that you are My disciples, if you love one another.'

Conclusion

The Scriptures prove beyond doubt that the Law of Moses was given for a limited period of time, for a specific purpose and only to a specific group of people. All Believers, Jews and Gentiles, now live under Christ's law, a law of love. Obedience to Christ's law is the result of salvation, and contributes nothing towards the gaining or keeping of salvation. Understanding the right relationship between the Christian, the Law of Moses and the law of Christ will:

i. Bring spiritual maturity	Heb. 5:13
ii. Bring fruit for the Gospel	Col. 1:6
iii. Give the Christian power over sin	1 Cor. 15:57
iv. Give Christians a new, and better, way of living	Gal. 6:2
v. Bring intimacy with God	Rom. 8:15

Let every Christian bring glory to Christ by living under His law, and His law alone.

CHAPTER 8

Forgiveness

'... a different gospel – which is really no gospel at all' (Gal. 1:6-7)

The Covenant which the Lord made with Israel, through Moses, was very much a covenant of obedience and works. The Covenant of Moses was a covenant under which man did something and then God responded. If man was obedient he was blessed by God; if man was disobedient, he was cursed and punished by God.

Jesus Christ brought in a New Covenant between God and man. It is a Covenant of grace not Law: a covenant of faith not works. From the very earliest times of the New Covenant, there has been a tendency to slip back into an Old Covenant style relationship with God. This has reached a stage now whereby many Christians believe that God is more pleased with them when they are 'doing well,' that somehow God loves the Christian more when he is striving to be 'a good Christian' and that God blesses Christians more when they are making every effort against sin.

Paul wrote to the Galatian church that he was astonished that they were so quickly deserting their calling and 'turning to a different gospel – which is really no gospel at all' (Gal. 1:6-7). For many today the Gospel has become not Good News at all. It has been transformed, by wrong teaching, into a confused, and confusing, mixture of good and bad news. Forgiveness is one of the fundamental areas of the Christian faith into which this wrong teaching has entered. The result is that many Christians now live with a man-centred understanding of forgiveness. This understanding brings back an Old Covenant relationship with God, which puts a heavy responsibility upon man, which robs the Christian of much of the 'joy of his salvation' and, above all, brings no glory to Jesus and all that He has achieved for the Believer.

Old Testament, Old Covenant, forgiveness

The Covenant of Moses, including the Ten Commandments, was a covenant relationship which depended upon obedience. Despite God's Word that He would curse and severely punish disobedience, Israel was repeatedly disobedient – as individuals and as a nation. God knew, when He gave Moses the Law, that Israel would continue to be disobedient. In order, therefore, to be able to maintain the Covenant relationship, God gave Israel the sacrificial system by which she might obtain forgiveness.

Under the Old Covenant forgiveness was something which man initiated and to which God then responded. Leviticus, chapters 4 and 5 detail some of the sacrifices to be made which would result in forgiveness. For example: Lev. 4:26, 'He [the priest] shall burn all the fat on the altar as he burned the fat of the fellowship offering. In this way the priest will make atonement for the man's sins, and he will be forgiven.' Another example is Lev. 6:7, 'In this way [the offering of a ram] the priest will make atonement for him [the sinner] before the Lord, and he will be forgiven for any of these things he did that make him guilty.'

So when a man needed to be forgiven he would bring the necessary sacrifice to the priest. The next step was that the priest would offer the sacrifice and make atonement and, once that was done, God forgave. So Old Covenant forgiveness was initiated by the sinner, carried though by the priest and then responded to by God.

Modern teaching

Modern teaching on forgiveness can often carry the same kind of Old Covenant message – in that it is something which man initiates, has to often repeat and to which God responds. Modern teaching on forgiveness can include these ideas:

Forgiveness is dependent upon confession of sin. This is based upon 1 John 1:9 which says, '*If* we confess our sins He [God] is faithful and just and will forgive us our sins...' (author's emphasis).

Christians are only forgiven if they forgive others. This is based upon Matt. 6:15 which says, 'But if you do not forgive men their sins, your Father will not forgive your sins.'

Forgiveness occurs on a moment by moment basis. Based upon Luke 17:4 which says, 'If he [your brother] sins against you seven times in a day, and seven times comes back to you and says, 'I repent' forgive him.'

Forgiveness is only given once it has been asked for. Based upon Matt. 6:12 which says, 'Forgive us our sins as we have forgiven those who sin against us.'

Christians must be baptized in order to be forgiven. This is based upon Acts 2:38 in which Peter tells the crowd, 'Repent and be baptized every one of you in the name of Jesus Christ so that your sins may be forgiven.'

Forgiveness is an act of grace on God's part. There is no Scriptural basis for this belief. It is rooted in a misunderstanding of God's dealings with man and the general sense of unworthiness which so often burdens Christians.

Not one of these modern teachings is true. Each teaching listed above leaves forgiveness as a man-initiated event – except for the last one which leaves God as someone who is gracious towards sin. All of the above teachings strike at the very heart of the Christian Gospel which is that, 'In the Gospel a righteousness [right standing with God] from God is revealed, a righteousness that is by faith from first to last, just as it is written: "The righteous will live by faith." ' (Rom. 1:17). In other words, the heart of the Christian Gospel is that faith in Christ, and that alone, is sufficient to make the Believer eternally right with God. This means that the Believer's sins are forgiven – for without that he cannot be right with God – as a result of faith, and faith alone.

The definition of forgiveness

One of the problems with a Christian's understanding of forgiveness is that there is a tendency to misuse the word in everyday conversation. When a person ask someone else to forgive him the word is generally being used it in the context of 'I am apologizing for what I have just done/said.' It can also be used to mean, 'Please don't be angry at me.' Another common use of the word is to convey the message, 'Please overlook the offence.' These modern misuses of the word 'forgive' are carried over into a

Christian's understanding of how God deals with sin and how God deals with the Christian. The Christian can often, in effect, be saying to God, 'I am apologizing for what I have done; please don't be angry with me. Please overlook the offence.' All of these are incorrect uses of the word. The phrase 'to forgive' comes from Greek and Hebrew words which have various applications and meanings. For example: it can be used in the sense of 'to atone or cover' and is used in this context in Rom. 3:25. The same root word is used in Matt. 18:27 where it speaks of a debt which was cancelled or pardoned. Another variation is to carry or take away and it is used in this way in John 1:29, 'Look, the Lamb of God who takes away the sin of the world.'

Two essential elements. There are the examples just listed and various other applications of the Greek and Hebrew words from which 'to forgive' originates. There are, though, two common elements which must be involved in the accurate use of the word 'forgiveness.' The two essential elements are: (i) the concept of the taking up of a burden created by someone else and (ii) the giving up of any resentment towards the one who created the burden. So when God says to man that He forgives men their sins He is, in effect, saying, 'I will bear the consequences of what you have done and I will not hold it against you.' Such a statement, such an understanding, contains the two elements of true forgiveness. God takes up the burden created by man's sins - the burden of the death penalty - and He does not hold that against man. He still extends His love and blessings towards man. Conversely, if a man asks God for forgiveness, he is saying to God, 'Please accept the burden created by my sin and do not hold it against me.'

God demands a death penalty for every sin - every bad thought, word and deed - ever committed by a person. An apology is not enough. God is angry about sin. God will always deal with sin as it deserves to be dealt with. God will never overlook sin or be lenient towards it. So, therefore, much of the way in which Christians use the word 'forgive' in relation to their sins is totally without effect, because many times the Christian is asking God to do something He cannot, and will not, do.

The most accurate definition, and demonstration, of forgiveness is the cross of Calvary. On that cross Jesus Christ accepted into Himself the penalty, the consequences, the burden, for the sins each person has committed, or will ever commit, and He did not, and does not, hold that against the sinner.

New Covenant forgiveness, correctly understood in this way, stands in stark contrast to Old Covenant forgiveness. No longer man-initiated, no longer man-centred, no longer often repeated. At Calvary it was God who initiated forgiveness by providing the sacrifice, it was God who was, and is, continually at the centre of the act of forgiveness as, in Jesus, He Himself became the means of atonement and it is a 'once for all' act which was concluded nearly 2,000 years ago. Any teaching, therefore, that the Christian still needs to bring 'sacrifices' – which today would be the asking for forgiveness, the forgiving of others, the confession of sin etc. – in order to receive forgiveness is completely wrong, and such a teaching is to imply that the sacrifice of Christ was insufficient to make the Believer eternally right with God.

The Christian's relationship with God

A Christian has, through Christ, been reconciled to God: 2 Cor. 5:19 says, 'God was reconciling the world to Himself in Christ, not counting men's sins against them.' The barrier of sin which once stood between God and man was dealt with by Jesus at the cross of Calvary. Now the Believer has been brought back into a family relationship with God in which the Believer is given the position, and rights, of a son. That relationship, once entered into, continues for eternity. The relationship with God is one which He offers to man as an outworking of His grace towards man. This means that the relationship is based upon the fundamental truth of grace which is that it is freely and undeservedly given which means, in keeping with the true nature of God's grace, that *the relationship exists without regard to sin*.

A relationship with God can only commence once every question of sin has been dealt with. God cannot be in relationship with someone who is still guilty of offences against Him. God accomplished this for man at the cross of Christ. The reason a Christian is able to have a relationship with God is because Jesus, on the cross, took into Himself, all the sin of all mankind forever. John the Baptist testified, 'Look, the Lamb of God who takes away the sin of the world' (John 1:29). The Christian's sins have been taken away from him. In 1 John 2:2 it states that it is not only the sins of the Christian that were taken away but, '. . . the sins of the whole world.' The blood of Christ has reconciled the Christian to God. Nothing can ever break that relationship. It is guaranteed by the Holy Spirit Himself. Eph. 1:13-14 says, 'Having believed, you were marked in Him with a seal, the promised Holy Spirit, who is a deposit guaranteeing our inheritance . . .' Therefore, with every question of sin dealt with by Jesus' sacrifice, 'once for all,' forgiveness cannot be given on a moment by moment, daily basis – otherwise the Christian's relationship with God would be equally 'on and off' Sadly that is exactly the kind of relationship which many Christians do have with God. Forgiveness was achieved for the Christian by Jesus. He bore the guilt for the Christian and took away all the sin.

The Christian's relationship with God, being based upon the fundamental truth of grace – that it is freely and undeservedly given – means, in keeping with the true nature of God's grace, that ***the relationship exists without regard to the response***.

The Christian's relationship with God cannot depend, in any way at all, on anything that the Christian does for God. If it does then it would mean that a Christian's relationship with God is not based upon His grace, but upon a mixture of His grace and the Christian's works. Grace has to be totally free of obligation in order to remain grace. Therefore forgiveness, without which the Christian cannot be in relationship with God, cannot depend upon anything the Christian does. The teachings about the need to confess sin, forgive others, ask for forgiveness and so on, as something man needs to do in order to be forgiven, would place man in a works-oriented relationship with God. Such an understanding stands opposed to Scripture which states, 'It is by grace you have been saved, through faith – and this not from yourselves, it is the gift of God – not by works, so that no-one can boast' (Eph. 2:8-9).

The Christian's relationship with God is based solely upon what

Christ has achieved for man. In Him the Christian is made right with God. It is Christ's achievement, freely given to the Believer, that makes the Believer acceptable to God. Nothing the Believer does, or does not do, can affect his standing before God. Therefore forgiveness, which is necessary for the relationship with God to start, must be dependent only upon faith in Christ - and His achievement on behalf of the Believer - not upon anything the Believer may do. This also reinforces the point that the Christian is forgiven once for all time. The Believer is forgiven of all sins at the moment of coming to faith in Christ - it is not, as under the Old Covenant, an often repeated event.

New Testament teaching on forgiveness

The purpose of looking at these Scriptures is to show that, under the New Covenant, forgiveness is now a Christ-initiated, Christ-oriented aspect of man's relationship with God.

Forgiveness is a debt cancelled. Matt. 18:23-27. The king in this story is owed a large amount of money. The debtor is unable to pay the debt. The man who owes the money seeks to be the author of his own salvation in that he offers, in verse 26, to pay back the king the debt that is owed. The king, in verse 27 demonstrates the Good News of Gospel, in that he realizes the man is not able to pay back the debt so, instead of accepting the offer from the man, the king cancels the debt. That is New Covenant forgiveness - a debt cancelled. The king accepted the burden created by the debtor and took the loss of the money, and the king did not hold it against the man because, after cancelling the debt, the king let the man go.

Forgiveness depends upon what Jesus has done for man. Matt. 26:28. Jesus, when instructing His followers at the last supper, said to them, 'This is My blood of the new covenant which is poured out for many for the forgiveness of sins.' Forgiveness, in the New Covenant, comes through the blood of Christ. Man contributes nothing towards it. It is impossible to add to, or take away from, the achievement of the blood of the Lamb. Understanding this truth should bring a Christian into a more stable, constant relationship with God. When a Christian understands that he or she is totally and utterly forgiven, and that through the blood of Jesus, it will better enable the Christian to experience the joy of their salvation. (See also: Eph. 1:7.)

Forgiveness is the result of faith – not a separate issue. Mark 2:1-12. The paralytic in this story was carried to Jesus by his friends and lowered through the roof. The passage says that, 'When Jesus saw their faith he said to the paralytic, "Son, your sins are forgiven."' At this point the paralytic and his friends have demonstrated only faith. The Scripture points that out - 'When Jesus saw their faith...' If forgiveness of sins depends upon anything other than faith then Jesus had no right to respond to their faith by pronouncing the man's sins forgiven. Jesus responded to their faith, and He responds to the Christian's faith – not his deeds or contribution. Forgiveness does not depend upon the Christian doing something, but on the Christian believing something.

Forgiveness is through faith. Luke 7:36-50. This is the story of the woman at the house of Simon the Pharisee. The woman, in serving Jesus, makes up for the shortcomings, and deliberate rudeness, of Simon towards Jesus. She demonstrates a great love for Jesus and carries out acts of service which involve her own humiliation before those present. In verse 48 Jesus tells the woman, 'Your sins are forgiven.' It is not the acts of service, though, which have brought that forgiveness, for in verse 50 Jesus says to the woman, 'Your faith has saved you.' Christians must proclaim the truth, that forgiveness comes only through faith in Jesus - not even through costly acts of humiliating service, as carried out by this woman. It is through faith, and faith alone that a person is made right with God.

Forgiveness empowers for service. Luke 7:41-43, 47-48. Jesus, in the same incident at Simon's house, tells Simon a parable about two debtors. One owes a large amount, the other owes a smaller amount. The one who is owed the money cancels the debt of both men because neither is able to pay back their debt. Jesus asks, 'Who will love the forgiving creditor more?' Simon answers correctly that the one who had the bigger debt cancelled will love the more. When a Christian realises that ALL his or her sins are forgiven, that the Christian eternally has a 'clean sheet' from the first moment of salvation, then that Christian will love God the more. That is the teaching of Scripture. The greater the awareness of forgiveness, the greater the love for the one forgiving. Jesus then tells Simon that He knows the woman's sins are forgiven, because she has shown much, and costly, love. In verse 48 Jesus says to the woman, 'Your sins are forgiven.' In the Greek that sentence is written in the perfect passive sense. What that means is that Jesus is recognizing in the woman a present condition that results from a past action. In other words, Jesus is saying, 'I know you have received forgiveness for your sins because I can see the great love you have shown Me.' It is a present condition resulting from something that has already occurred. Both the parable of the two debtors, and Jesus' conversation with the woman, make the very important point that the receiving of forgiveness empowers the Christian, through the love he or she has for the One who forgives, into acts of service – even costly service. 'He who has been forgiven little, loves little,' said Jesus. Little love brings little service. Let all Christians receive the freely offered forgiveness of God, and through the power of their greater love for the One who forgives, go on and serve the One who died in order to be able to give that forgiveness.

Forgiveness is a free gift. Luke 15:11-24. In the story of the prodigal son, the father demonstrates New Covenant forgiveness. On seeing the son returning, the father further humiliates himself by running through the village to meet the son. In the Middle East no man would consider running in public as it is considered undignified. This father, though, is thinking only of his son. The father asks no questions of the son, makes no demands of the son, puts no conditions upon the son, gives no rebuke to the son. The father overwhelms the son with love and a free offer of restoration to sonship. The son had come back with the attitude of a servant – he was going to work for his father. Freely offered forgiveness changed the young man from a servant to a son. It does the same for the Christian. The father bore the burden created by his son, and did not hold that against the son. That is New Covenant forgiveness.

Forgiveness is a work of God for man, not a work of man for God. Luke 18:9-14. The Pharisee more than kept the Law. He was a man more than dedicated to doing what God required. The Law required that the Pharisee fast once a week – this Pharisee fasted twice a week. The Law required a tenth of agricultural produce – this Pharisee gave a tenth of everything he had. The tax collector offered no such strivings, or good works, to God. He simply asked that God would have mercy on him – the phrase used in the Scriptures means, literally, 'Lord, make atonement for me.' The tax collector went home, Jesus said, justified. His sins were forgiven though the atoning sacrifice of Christ, not through his contribution – except the faith that trusted God to do for him what he could not do for himself.

Forgiveness does not depend upon what man does. Luke 23:34. As Jesus was being nailed to the cross He prayed, 'Father, forgive them, for they do not know what they are doing.' To understand forgiveness correctly, the question must be asked, 'By what right did Jesus ask the Father to forgive His murderers?' It was a murder because the High Priest, the Pharisees and the Romans all knew that Jesus had, in the words of Pontius Pilate, committed no crime that warranted the death penalty. If much of modern teaching on forgiveness is correct then Jesus had no right to ask the Father to forgive His murderers. They had not confessed to their act as a sin, they had not asked for forgiveness nor had they expressed any sorrow for their actions. None of the things which, in fact, many Christians are told are necessary before God will grant forgiveness. The reason Jesus did have a right to make that request of His Father was because He was about to accept into Himself the consequences of their action and He was not holding that against them – and those are the two elements of true forgiveness. Forgiveness is never deserved – as this Scripture clearly shows. Forgiveness is a work of God for man, not the other way round. Forgiveness is freely offered, faith opens the Christian up to receive what is offered. Nailed to the cross by a jeering, Christ-rejecting crowd, He prays for His murderers, 'Father, forgive them.' That is true New Covenant forgiveness. It is Christ bearing the burden of man's sins and not holding it against them. By the grace of God, that same freely offered, undeserved forgiveness is still available to all today who will only believe.

Forgiveness is through faith in Jesus, and that alone. Luke 23:42-43. Surely one of the clearest examples of forgiveness through faith, and faith alone, must be the thief dying on the cross alongside Jesus. The thief did absolutely nothing except place his hope, his faith, in Jesus Christ. That was sufficient for Jesus to reassure him of his salvation – which entails and includes his forgiveness. If a declaration of faith was sufficient for the thief, it must be sufficient for all men.

Forgiveness is a gift from God. Acts 5:31. 'God exalted Him [Jesus] to His own right hand as Prince and Saviour that He might GIVE repentance and forgiveness of sins to Israel' (author's emphasis). Forgiveness is a gift from Jesus. A gift is free. A gift is not contributed towards, not earned and not deserved; it is simply a gift. Jesus is the only One who can offer forgiveness of sins because it was He who bore the consequences. Since Calvary He has been saying to man, 'I have borne the consequences of what you have done and I do not hold that against you.' Man is required only to believe the Good News.

Forgiveness depends only upon faith. Acts 10:43. Here is another Scripture which makes plain the simple truth that forgiveness comes through faith in Christ, and that alone. Forgiveness is not a burden to be carried by the Christian. An understanding of forgiveness makes it one of the sources of joy in a Christian's life and relationship with God. Another free gift! This Scripture says, 'All the prophets testify about Him [Jesus] that everyone who believes in Him receives forgiveness of sins through His name.' Faith and forgiveness are not separate issues. If a Christian has faith in Jesus, that Christian is forgiven. This right understanding reinforces the central truth of Christian teaching which is that faith, and faith alone, is all that is required of man by God. (See also: Acts 13:38-39.)

Forgiveness is not contributed to by man in any way. Col. 2:13. This Scripture says, 'When you were dead in your sins and in the uncircumcision of your sinful nature, God made you alive with Christ. He forgave us all our sins . . .' This makes it clear that

FORGIVENESS

forgiveness is something God has done for man. It is so important to stress this point because so much of what is taught as the Gospel reverses this emphasis and stresses what man should be doing for God. Such teaching is neither the Gospel nor Good News and makes Christ's burden heavy, contrary to His own words, in Matt. 11:30, '... My burden is light.' Wrong teaching has caused their faith to be a heavy burden for many Christians. Forgiveness in the New Covenant is a source of great joy for the Believer.

Forgiveness is dependent upon the shedding of blood. Heb. 9:22. 'In fact, the law requires that nearly everything be cleansed with blood, and without the shedding of blood there is no forgiveness.' Those who teach that forgiveness is dependent upon a contribution from man overlook this Scripture and have a cheap and easy forgiveness. God has always demanded a blood sacrifice for forgiveness. Forgiveness does not come on the basis of a prayer request, nor on the basis of a confession of sin, nor on the basis of expressing sorrow. Forgiveness does not come on the basis of making every effort not to sin again, nor on the basis of any other of these modern day sacrifices that Christians are often encouraged to bring to God. Forgiveness comes on the basis of shed blood. For the Israelites that meant animal sacrifices, but for the Christian it means the blood of Christ. It is that, and that alone, that allows God to forgive man's sins. This Scripture shows that God granted forgiveness to man nearly 2,000 years ago, when the blood was shed, and not on a daily basis as the sin occurs. Christ is not shedding His blood today. Forgiveness is no longer an issue between God and the Believer. As Christ proclaimed, 'It is finished.' In 1 John 2:12 the apostle writes, 'I write to you, dear children, because your sins have been forgiven on account of His name.' John uses the past tense, it has already happened.

Not understanding forgiveness as a past event leads to ineffectiveness for the Gospel. 2 Peter 1:5-9. Peter has been writing about the different qualities a Christian should seek to build up in his or her life. In verse 8, Peter writes that possession of these qualities, which include faith, goodness, knowledge, self-control and others leading up to love, will prevent a Christian 'being ineffective and unproductive in [their] knowledge of our

Lord Jesus Christ.' In verse 9 Peter writes, 'But if anyone does not have them, he is near-sighted and blind, and has forgotten that he has been cleansed from his past sins.' Forgetting that forgiveness is a closed issue, forgetting that all past sins (and the past starts now!) have been forgiven will lead a Christian to be ineffective for the Gospel. This will happen because the Christian will assume that his daily life continually presents a barrier between him and God. Such a Christian will not expect much from God and, as Jesus experienced in Nazareth, God will be able to work little through such a Believer because of their lack of faith – not in God's power, but faith in their standing before God.

Forgiveness is justice, not grace. 1 John 1:9. Through lack of understanding many Believers think that God's forgiveness is an act of grace from Him to the Believer. It is not. This Scripture states clearly that when 'we confess [that is, agree with God about] our sins then He is faithful and JUST and will forgive us our sins . . .' (author's emphasis). God will always punish sin. His grace is that He sent His Son to be the punishment bearer. Having thus punished Jesus in our stead, God, in not punishing man for his sins, is simply acting in a just way. There is no punishment due the sinner, that is why he is not punished. It is fair, it is just, but it is not grace. Jesus is God's grace to man. This is more than any apparent semantics, or splitting of hairs. It has to do with the Believers' basic attitude to forgiveness and, thus, to God. Forgiveness, for the Believer in Christ, is a right; not an act of Divine mercy. The Believer should be confident in what Christ has achieved for him. (Heb. 4:16).

Two questions

Hebrews 10:1 says, 'The Law is only a shadow of the good things that are coming – not the realities themselves. For this reason it can never, by the same sacrifices repeated endlessly year after year, make perfect those who draw near to worship.'

The sacrifices offered to obtain forgiveness had to be endlessly repeated. Each new sin demanded a new sacrifice in order to receive new forgiveness – that is the declared way of things under the Old Covenant of Moses.

Under the New Covenant, though, the Bible declares, in Hebrews 10:12-14, 'But when this priest [Jesus] had offered for all time one sacrifice for sins, He sat down at the right hand of God. Since that time He waits for His enemies to be made His footstool, because by one sacrifice He has made perfect forever those who are being made holy.' What a joyful contrast to the old Covenant! In Christ, and by Christ, the Believer has been made perfect in the sight of God. The Believer may not feel or think he is perfect, but the Word of God stands far above human feelings and thoughts. Repeated sacrifices brought no perfection, but the one sacrifice of Christ brought perfection to the Believer. *The first question is: **If Christ has made the Believer perfect, as the Bible says, in the eyes of God, then how can the Believer continually need to be forgiven?***

Col. 1:22 says, 'But now He [God] has reconciled you by Christ's physical body through death to present you holy in His sight, without blemish and free from accusation.' *The second question is: **If the Believer is free, through Christ, even from accusation, then how can the Believer possibly need to be forgiven of anything?***

Conclusion

The contrast between old Covenant and New Covenant forgiveness is clear:

Old Testament, Old Covenant forgiveness	New Testament, New Covenant forgiveness
Repeated sacrifices	One sacrifice
Man provided the sacrifice	Christ provided the sacrifice
Works	Faith
The priest made atonement	Christ made atonement
Brought no perfection	Brings perfection
God forgave	God forgave

All the Scriptures listed (as well as many others), the death and resurrection of Jesus Christ, the indwelling Holy Spirit and the Believer's new, and eternal, relationship with God, all testify to the following truths about forgiveness in the New Covenant:

Forgiveness: is something done by God for man;
     comes through faith, and faith, alone;
     is a gift from God;
     is a 'once for all' event;
     is an act of justice, not grace.

Only with such an understanding of forgiveness can the Scripture be true which says, in Rom. 5:1, 'Therefore, since we have been justified through faith, we have peace with God through our Lord Jesus Christ.'

CHAPTER 9

Obedience

Introduction
When grace is preached, or taught, in all its purity it is not uncommon to hear a response that the message is one which allows the Christian to do anything he or she wants, with no regard to the need for obedience. Someone once said, 'If what you are preaching cannot be mistaken for licence, then you are probably not preaching the Gospel.' The truth is that the Gospel contains such unlimited freedom that there will always be a risk that, when accurately preached, it may be misunderstood as licence. Indeed, this very reason was the cause of many a conflict between Jesus and the Pharisees, who thought that Jesus had a decidedly casual attitude towards the Law and towards sin.

Christians, for a variety of reasons, back away from embracing grace in all its fullness. One of the reasons for this hesitancy is the fear of falling into licence. The hearts of such Christians are right, in that they wish to serve God through lives which honour Him in the way they are lived. Despite, though, their good desires to serve God, Biblically it is their very holding back from receiving grace that prevents them from seeing those heart desires fulfilled. Another reason why Christians hold back from embracing grace is that confusion exists between obligation and responsibility - which is one of the issues that will be addressed in this chapter. A third major reason for Christians holding back from living in grace is that there is also confusion within the Church about what exactly is the 'Rule of life' for a Christian, how should that Rule of life be achieved and the consequences, or otherwise, of Christians failing to achieve that Rule of life.

The result of this fear, confusion, misteaching and lack of understanding is that the Believer becomes an ineffective witness for the Gospel. The Believer is left unsure of exactly what is the

Good News that should be proclaimed. The message becomes a mixture of Good News and not-so-good news, a mix of grace and Law, faith and works, with a resulting intermittent, seesaw relationship with God. It is not uncommon to find Christians living without any real peace in their relationship with God and without an absolute assurance of their salvation.

This fear, confusion, misteaching and lack of understanding also leads to division within the Church. One part of the Church, currently a small part, embraces grace and lives under grace; another part, currently the majority, rejects whole-hearted embracing of grace - for the reasons previously stated. Each rejects the teachings of the other. The confusion and division are irreconcilable - as grace and Law must always be - and the non-Christian is left even more confused and unreachable.

The purpose of this chapter is to look at, and answer, five basic questions. They are:

I. Is the Christian under an obligation to be obedient to God?
II. If there is no obligation, then why should the Christian bother to even try and be obedient - in other words, is not licence the inevitable result of living under grace?
III. To what, if anything, should the Christian seek to be obedient?
IV. How is the Christian expected, if at all, to be obedient?
V. What are the consequences if a Christian is not obedient?

I. Is the Christian under an obligation to be obedient to God?

The answer to this most fundamental, and crucial, question is, quite simply, 'No.' There is no doubt or confusion - it is clearly and unarguably, 'No.' Most Christians will be horrified at such an answer and, primarily out of fear of offending God, will pull back from daring to embrace this truth. The fundamental truth of grace - outlined in the first chapter of this book - is that grace, in order to be grace, must be free. The gift of Jesus, the eternal life that comes through His death and resurrection, and all the blessings poured out on the Christian through Jesus are all outworkings of God's grace. Which means that they are all freely given. If a Believer picks up any obligation as a result of what God has done for man, then God's work on man's behalf ceases to be grace and becomes simply an exchange – God's saving work in exchange, in this case, for man's obedience. A mass of Scriptures testify that the Believer is saved by grace and that God's grace is freely given. If these numerous Scriptures are true – which, of course, they are – then man can never be placed under *any* obligation or condition as a result of what God has done. That lack of obligation must, very obviously, include a lack of obligation to be obedient.

The child of God has been set free. Galatians 5:1 says, 'It is for freedom that Christ has set us free.' The purpose in Christ setting the Christian free was that the Christian might live in that freedom. In Scripture there is no limit given, by which the Christian may enhance his standing before God, to what the Bible terms '. . . the glorious freedom of the children of God.' (Rom. 8:21). In terms of the Christian's standing before God, he may do what he wants, when he wants, with whom he wants, how he wants and where he wants. This is the boundless freedom, and unlimited security, which Christ purchased for the Believer at Calvary. It is the very boundless nature of this freedom that scares Christian into not embracing it. It sounds too much like licence. To avoid this supposed licence, and due to lack of understanding of the empowering nature of grace, Christians, individually and as churches and denominations, begin to impose rules. Those rules then become a burden to many a weaker Christian. Yet careful examination of the Scriptures reveal that those rules have no Biblical mandate. In fact, the same Scripture, Galatians 5:1, which speaks of the freedom of the Believer in Christ, urges the Believer, 'Stand firm, then, and do not let yourselves be burdened again by a yoke of slavery.' That 'yoke' is the same one which Peter spoke against in Acts 15:10 when he spoke against those who were seeking to compel Gentile Believers to obey the Law of Moses.

II. If there is no obligation, why should the Christian bother to even try and be obedient – in other words, is not licence the inevitable result of living under grace?

Those who argue that embracing the boundless freedom of Christ will inevitably lead to licence, do not understand the difference between obligation and responsibility. An obligation is compulsory whereas responsibility, although the best course of action, remains a matter of individual choice. Responsibility fits in with a Gospel of grace, obligation does not.

The Apostle Paul sets the context within which the many commands for holy living under the New Covenant are given. In 1 Corinthians 6:12 Paul writes, 'Everything is permissible for me' - but not everything is beneficial.' This reinforces the concept of the unlimited freedom of Christ. An amazing thing about Christians is that they will proclaim a Scripture, believing with all their heart in the unchallengeable truth of God's Holy Word, and then they will immediately contradict that Scripture. 1 Corinthians 6:12 is a good example of this. Christians will declare, with Paul, that 'Everything is permissible...' but will then immediately follow that up by listing what, in reality - at least in their confused opinion - is NOT permissible. 'Everything is permissible...' declares the Bible - '...but you cannot have sex before marriage,' responds the Christian. 'Everything is permissible...' proclaims God's Word - '...but you cannot get drunk,' choruses the Christian. And so the confused teaching goes on. People who believe totally in the Bible as God's inspired and Holy Word will not hesitate, due to lack of understanding of grace, to contradict it when to accept it would appear to be licence - as though the Word itself would encourage licence! Not only does the concept of grace demand limitless freedom but in 1 Corinthians 6:12, and other places, the Bible spells out clearly that there truly is limitless freedom in Christ.

Having proclaimed the fundamental truth that, in keeping with a Gospel of grace, everything is permissible, Paul then goes on in the same verse to unfold the reasons why recklessly embracing that limitless freedom may not be beneficial. There are three reasons that Paul gives as justification for a self-imposed restriction on the way Christians live. The first is revealed in the second part of 1 Corinthians 6:12. The verse continues, 'Everything is permissible for me - but I will not be mastered by anything.' The first reason that Paul gives for not exercising the complete freedom that he has in Christ is that he, Paul, does not want to be mastered by anything. It is not at all unwise for the Christian to limit the freedom that God gives him; but the limitation is imposed for the benefit of the Christian and other people. Any such limitation in no way enhances the Christian's standing before God or contributes to the assurance of his salvation. If a Christian has a sinful habit in which he or she indulges – safe in the knowledge that all sin is paid for – that habit will soon become one which has an irresistible power and the Christian, through ignoring God's Word, will find himself 'mastered' by that habit. Paul points out in this verse that it is not of benefit to the individual Christian to engage in limitless freedom to the extent that he or she actually ends up losing some of that freedom. However, there is no obligation imposed through this verse. The Believer is advised of the correct course of action and, then, left with the free will choice of whether to follow that advice. That whole scenario agrees with the Gospel of grace. It does not have to be an obviously sinful habit which gains mastery. Limitless freedom includes the freedom to impose restrictions. It could be an often repeated religious restriction or exercise which, eventually, detracts from the joy and peace with God which rightfully belong to the Christian and, being thus not beneficial, is an incorrect use of the freedom of the Believer. In 1 Corinthians 8:9 Paul gives the second reason why the Christian should willingly put a restriction upon their freedom. The Scripture says, 'Be careful, however, that the exercise of your freedom does not become a stumbling block to the weak.' Once again, this restriction fits in comfortably with the Gospel of grace. The restriction is put forward by Paul for the benefit of other people. If the exercise of a sinful habit, or the exercise of a legalistic ritual or restriction, is seen by a weaker Believer, or by a non-Believer, as legitimizing such activity then it should be given up. So the restriction is for the purpose of being a better witness and example. There is no compulsion in this advice. It is the correct thing to do – live in such a way that does not cause a weaker person to stumble – but it a matter of individual choice as to whether that advice is followed. Equally there is no suggestion that the following, or not following, of this advice will in any way affect the Believer's standing before God.

In 1 Corinthians 10:23 Paul gives the third reason for the Christian self-imposing a restriction upon his otherwise unlimited freedom. Paul writes: '"Everything is permissible" – but not everything is beneficial. "Everything is permissible" – but not everything is constructive.'

Within this letter to the Corinthians, Paul writes four times the phrase 'Everything is permissible.' It is a generally accepted principle of Bible study that when the Bible repeats something it is because God considers is especially important. Here is a repeat of the repeat! It seems almost as though God knew what a struggle His people would have in accepting the boundless freedom He gives them and, therefore, He stresses – four times in all – 'Everything is permissible.' There is such freedom in that truth for any Believer who is struggling with some sinful habit or desire. Such freedom for the non-Christian who holds back from embracing the faith because of activities or thought patterns which they feel – and may even have been taught – will make them unacceptable to God.

In 1 Corinthians 10:23 Paul says that, although everything is permissible, not everything is constructive; and in verse 24 he goes on to explain in what way some things are not constructive. He writes, 'Nobody should seek his own good, but the good of others.' An individual Christian's maturity and personal relationship with God may allow that Christian to live in a certain way; but, if another sees that lifestyle and, perhaps by copying it, is harmed by it then the freedom enjoyed by the stronger Christian is now, in these circumstances, no longer constructive – but potentially destructive. This again is a self-imposed restriction which is in keeping with grace. It is a choice the stronger Christian makes based upon helping others, and not upon enhancing his standing before God.

Living, therefore, under grace will not lead to licence. Of course there is a right way to live as a Christian; but it is a matter of free choice as to whether the individual Believer lives in that right way. Whether or not a Christian does live 'the right way' will not affect the Christian's standing before God – although recklessly embracing freedom may actually lead to a loss of freedom (being 'mastered' by something) and to being a bad witness who causes others to stumble.

If a Christian is living according to the Word of God, that Christian will not end up with a set of rules and regulations of what he or she can and cannot do; but, that Christian will receive guidance on why his or her freedom should, on occasion, be voluntarily curtailed. That might almost sound like splitting hairs – to say, when the result is the same, that a Christian is choosing to be obedient to God's Word rather than being compelled to obey; but, in reality, it is a most fundamental difference. It is the difference between grace and Law. It is the difference that can bring freedom, peace and joy to any Christian struggling to be obedient. It is a difference that removes all pressure from the Believer. This, in turn, deepens the love the Believer has for God – a God who is now making no demands, but is truly accepting that Believer exactly as he or she is. As the love a Believer has for God deepens, amazing things begin to happen. Jesus Christ said, 'If you love Me, you will obey what I command' (John 14:15). The sequence is to love God first, then – and the Believer has Christ's promise on the matter – the obedience will follow. Christians today must get that sequence in the right order and must work on falling in love with Christ.

III. To what if anything, should the Christian seek to be obedient?

Having established that there is no obligation to be obedient, but that a Christian nevertheless has a responsibility to live in a certain way, the question arises: 'To what should the Christian seek to be obedient?' The first thing to recognize is that there are two areas within which Christian obedience applies. It is vitally important to recognize these two areas and to put them in the correct order of priority. The areas are: (i) spiritual obedience and (ii) practical obedience. The tendency in much modern teaching is to emphasize practical obedience without teaching that this can only flow subsequent to spiritual obedience.

(i) Spiritual obedience

In John 6:28 Jesus was asked, 'What must we do to do the works God requires?' The answer given by Jesus in the subsequent verse gives only one 'work' that is required by God. Jesus said, 'The work of God is this: to believe in the One He has sent.' They came looking for a list – 'the works' God requires; Jesus gave them one task, to believe. John emphasizes this point in 1 John 3:23. He writes, 'And this is His command: to believe in the name of His Son, Jesus Christ, and to love one another as He commanded us.' This is the priority and the sequence – faith, and then the outworking of that faith.

It might appear that there is a conflict here with grace, because there is now an obligation – an obligation to have faith. However, this does not create conflict within a Gospel of grace – which cannot, by definition, impose any obligation – because in Ephesians 2:8 it is written that God Himself gives the Believer the faith needed for salvation. So, yes, faith is a requirement; but, in keeping with grace, God meets that requirement for the Believer: 'For it is by grace you have been saved, through faith – and this not from yourselves, it is the gift of God...' Eph. 2:8. The question being examined is: 'To what should the Christian be obedient?' In the first area, of spiritual obedience, the requirement is, 'Have faith.' As God gives the Believer the faith that God requires, then every Believer is, obviously, obedient to the fundamental requirement of God as expressed by His Son in John 6:29. An examination of the Scriptures shows just how much that God-given faith achieves for the Believer. Acts 26:18 says the Believer is sanctified by faith, Romans 1:17 (also: Rom. 3:22, Rom. 4:5, Rom. 9:30) says that a Believer is made righteous through faith and Romans 5:1 says the Believer is justified through faith. Faith saves, justifies, counts as righteousness and sanctifies the Believer. Faith is God-given. Having given the Christian faith, God then counts that faith as obedience.

The Scriptures reinforce the truth that having faith and being obedient are the same thing by showing that God counts lack of faith as disobedience. In John 3:18, when speaking about faith in Jesus, it says, '... whoever does not believe stands condemned already because he has not believed ...' Lack of faith in Jesus is given as the only reason for condemnation under the New Covenant. In Romans 9:32 Paul writes that Israel failed to achieved righteousness because 'they pursued it not by faith but as if it were by works.' Romans 14:23 puts it very simply that, '... everything that does not come from faith is sin.' In Hebrews 3:18-19 the writer is addressing the issue of faith and obedience, which were more readily seen as synonymous in the early church than they are today. The writer asks the question, 'And to whom did God swear that they would never enter His rest if not to those who disobeyed? So we see that they were not able to enter, because of their unbelief.' These verses in particular clearly link disobedience and disbelief. So the primary requirement of God, in terms of obedience, is that of faith. If a person has faith, which is given by God, then God counts that person as saved, justified, righteous and sanctified.

(ii) Practical obedience

The Scriptures provide a mass of evidence that the Christian is not under the Law of Moses. In this book that subject is covered in greater detail in the chapter entitled, 'The Commandments and The Christian.' Sufficient here to quote just two Scriptures to briefly make the point. In Acts 15 Peter is addressing the issue of whether or not Gentile Believers should be required to be circumcised and obey the Law of Moses. In verse 9-11 Peter says, 'He [God] made no distinction between us and them [the Gentiles], for He purified their hearts by faith. Now then, why do you try to test God by putting on the necks of the disciples a yoke [circumcision and the Law] that neither we nor our fathers have been able to bear? No! We believe it is through the grace of our Lord Jesus that we are saved, just as they are.' Peter clearly rebukes those who would put Christians under the Law of Moses. Hebrews 7:12 gives the background as to why. It says, 'For when there is a change of the priesthood, there must also be a change of the law.' With Christ the priesthood changed. No longer did Aaron and his descendants fulfil the role of High Priest of Israel – although Israel herself did not understand this truth – for now, as Hebrews 3:1 and other Scriptures make clear, Jesus Christ is the eternal High

Priest for all Believers. Paul gives title to the new law which started with the new priesthood. In 1 Corinthians 9:20-21 he writes. 'To those under the law I became like one under the law (though I myself am not under the law), so as to win those under the law. To those not having the law I became like one not having the law (though I am not free from God's law but am under *Christ's law*) . . .' (author's emphasis). This then is the name of the Rule of Life or Law, which applies to the Christian. The Christian is not obliged to obey it, but it is beneficial for the Christian, and others, if he or she does so.

The nature of Christ's law

Paul, it may be remembered, wrote in 1 Corinthians 6:12, 'Everything is permissible for me but I will not be mastered by anything.' The paradox of obeying Christ's law and self-limiting personal freedom is that it gives greater freedom. By willingly surrendering freedom there is no loss of freedom to some enslaving habit. This glorious truth about Christ's law is testified to in James 1:25 where he writes, 'But the man who looks intently into the perfect law that gives freedom . . .' What joy there is in that Scripture for every Believer! A law which gives freedom. Not the heavy yoke which Israel was unable to bear. Not the Law by which '. . . we were held prisoners . . .' (Gal. 3:23). The Christian should seek to be obedient to a law, or rule of life, which enhances and strengthens his or her freedom. That fits in with the Gospel of grace and with the mission of Christ – as that is expressed in Galatians 5:1 It will help the Christian determine which law he or she is following if the question is asked: 'Is this law, this rule of life, under which I am living the liberating law of Christ or the heavy yoke of the enslaving Law of the Old Covenant of Moses?' Christ's law is a law of love. In 1 Corinthians 16:14 Paul directs the Christian, 'Do everything in love.' That is the reason for a Christian living by Christ's law – that love may be pre-eminent. This again provides a useful measure of which law, and therefore which Covenant, the Christian is living under. Is love the motivation for what the Christian is, or is not, doing. If it is not, then that Christian is not under Christ's law.

Christ's law is a law which is concerned first and foremost with the well-being of others. In Galatians 6:2 Paul directs the Christian to, 'Carry each other's burdens . . .' and goes on to say, '. . . and in this way you will fulfil the law of Christ.' This fits in completely with the mission and example of Jesus and is another guide as to which law the Christian is following. None of the revealed purposes of Christ's law is to enhance the standing of the Christian before God; they are all to do with bettering the lot of the Christian's fellow men and women. Christ Himself testified that, 'All men will know you are My disciples, if you love one another' (John 13:35). Jesus said that 'My yoke is easy and My burden is light' (Matt. 11:30) and John confirms this in 1 John 5:3 when he writes, '. . . His commands are not burdensome.'

In summary, that to which a Christian should seek to be obedient is the law of Christ. It is a law which brings freedom, which is motivated by love, which is primarily concerned about the well-being of others and which is not a heavy load. If those conditions are not fulfilled then, no matter what the motivation, any supposed obedience is outside of the law of Christ and, as such, has no Biblical mandate.

IV. How is the Christian expected, if at all, to be obedient?

So far it has been established that there is no obligation to be obedient, but there is a responsibility to live a right and that this is achieved by adhering to the law of Christ. The next issue, for the Christian who wishes to follow his Master, is 'How is a Christian expected to be obedient?' This is a very important question because if the Christian is simply left with his own strength and good intentions then he is in no different a position to the Israelites living under the Covenant of Moses. What is the difference for the Christian? How can the Christian stop the law of Christ becoming a burden? What hope, and peace, is there for the Christian who seems to be forever failing to live by the law of Christ?

The fundamental truth about the Covenant of Grace, the New Covenant in Christ's blood, is that it is all about what God has done, is doing and will do for man. This, obviously, includes the area of obedience. At no point, under the New Covenant, is the Christian ever called upon to do anything in his or her own strength.

God's equipping of the Christian includes faith, the Holy Spirit, grace, love and, of course, Jesus Himself. Five gifts which God has given to Believers by which they may live out the life to which they have been called.

Faith

In Romans 1:5 Paul writes, 'Through Him and for His name's sake we received grace and apostleship to call people from among all the Gentiles to the obedience that comes from faith.' The Christian is called to an obedience that springs from faith. This is not the obedience of striving and never-ending resolutions to do better. This is not the obedience of trying to be someone, or something, that in reality has not yet been achieved. The Christian is essentially called to an obedience that says, 'I can – because God says I can.' If that kind of faith is not present for any given issue then all that is left is striving. That striving, because it is not empowered by God-given faith, is a complete waste of time – as many a frustrated and despondent Christian will testify. There are many Scriptures which make this point: 1 Corinthians 16:13, '. . . stand firm in the faith'; 2 Corinthians 1:24, 'It is by faith you stand firm.' 1 Thessalonians 1:3 speaks of '. . . your work produced by faith.' Everywhere the emphasis is upon what the Christian will achieve through faith. That includes the ability to be obedient. That faith is a gift from God so, in keeping with the Covenant of Grace, Christian obedience becomes God's responsibility. That takes all the pressure off the Christian, and opens the Christian up to being more obedient.

The Holy Spirit

Salvation is a gift of God which contains many aspects. For some Christians, salvation means, basically, that they will not go to hell when they die. Yet salvation in reality means so much more. Amongst other things, salvation means a daily relationship with

God. That is brought about through the gift of the Holy Spirit. The Christian will become obedient to the law of Christ because he or she has the indwelling Holy Spirit, one of whose tasks is to bring about that obedience. Romans 15:16 speaks of the fact that the Gentile Believers have become acceptable to God, having been 'sanctified by the Holy Spirit.' It is the Spirit's job to bring about the sanctification of the Believer. That is Good News! No more striving; no more sense of failure, of letting God down. Now the Believer's sanctification is God's responsibility. Philippians 2:13 states that, '...it is God who works in you to will and act according to His good purpose.' Once again, when properly examined, the Scriptures reveal that God places no burden upon the Believer but, instead, accepts Himself the responsibility for making the Believer acceptable to Himself. Another task of the Holy Spirit, according to Jesus, is to lead the Believer into a knowledge of all truth (John 16:13). Part of the truth the Spirit will reveal is that the Believer is not under Law. The Scriptures say that '...the power of sin is the law.' (1 Corinthians 15:56). If the Believer is freed from the power of the Law then that Believer is freed from the power of sin. That is the Word of God, and the Spirit will guide the Believer into that truth. The Law does not have power to make the Believer sin; the Law has power - of guilt and failure - to make the Believer withdraw from communion with God, the very source of his or her strength and help when sin persists in the life of the Believer. The Spirit will encourage life-giving fellowship between the Believer and God by showing that the Believer is acceptable to God at all times, because of Jesus.

Grace
Sadly many Christians think that grace is an easy option, an alternative to obedience. This is dealt with in greater depth in another chapter. The Scriptures make it clear that the opposite is true, in that grace is the very source of Christian obedience. Romans 5:17 says, in the second half of the verse, '...how much more will those who receive God's abundant provision of grace and of the gift of righteousness reign in life through the one man, Jesus Christ.' This Scripture makes it very clear that it is the

receiving of grace which allows the Christian to reign in life. It is not by striving that greater victories will come, it is by receiving grace. That goes against human wisdom – how can more be achieved by making less effort? Believers are not encouraged to make less effort, God simply directs them to where their effort should go. Christians should put their effort into receiving grace, and the gift of God-given righteousness, and through that they will reign in life. Romans 5:2 speaks of 'this grace in which we now stand.' It is by grace the Believer will stand. That grace is entered into, as Romans 5:2 also states, not by striving but 'by faith.' Grace is the source of hard work in the life of a Believer – as both 1 Corinthians 15:10 and 2 Corinthians 9:8 make clear. Grace, then, is another provision which God has made by which the Believer will be enabled to live out the Christian life.

Love
Love is the law under which the Christian lives. Love is the command of Jesus Christ – John 15:12 and elsewhere. Love is the source of obedience in the life of a Christian. In John 14:15 Jesus says, 'If you love Me, you will obey what I command.' Once again God is redirecting the effort of the well-meaning Christian. It is not striving against sinful habits and passions that will get the Christian very far, it is falling in love with Jesus that makes the difference. That is the Word of God – and that is Good News! The sequence is love, then obedience. Even this love, God has provided for the Believer. Romans 5:5 says that '... God has poured out His love into our hearts by the Holy Spirit whom He has given us.' This is all entirely in keeping with the New Covenant which is all about God's provision for man. At no point, in the Scriptures' teachings on obedience under the New Covenant, does God point the Believer to himself and his own effort. Jesus says, 'Love Me and you will obey Me' and then God gives us His love in our hearts. In 1 Thessalonians 1:3 Paul commends the church there for '... your labour prompted by love ...;' The Bible says that 'God is love' (1 John 4:16). Love is the most powerful motivating force known to man. Love is the source of Christian obedience. Any other motivation is doomed to be short-lived and to end in failure. The

Christian should receive the love God has for him, the love God has given him, and allow that to flow through his or her life into acts of obedience – which, in accordance with the law of Christ, will primarily manifest as acts of caring for others.

Jesus Christ
Responsibility for a Christian's obedience falls squarely onto the shoulders of the Lord Jesus Christ. In Romans 14:4 Paul asks the question, 'Who are you to judge someone else's servant? To his own master he stands or falls. And he will stand, for the Lord is able to make him stand.' There is the promise of Holy Scripture that, despite any shortcomings, weaknesses, sinful habits and so on that may be in that Believer's life, he will stand – because Jesus Himself will make that Believer stand. The joyful news is that ultimate responsibility for the spiritual security of every Believer rests not with the Believer but with the Son of God. And that's very Good News! Philippians 4:13 also points to Jesus as the source of Christian strength, 'I can do everything through Him who gives me strength' and 1 Timothy 1:12 says, 'I thank Christ Jesus our Lord, who has given me strength...' It is Christ's task to ensure the security of each Believer and to empower him or her to live the life to which the Christian is called.

V. What are the consequences if a Christian is not obedient?
Under the Old Covenant the punishment for disobedience was clearly spelled out in Deuteronomy 28. God effectively told Israel, 'If you obey Me, I will bless you; if you disobey Me, I will curse every aspect of your personal, communal and national life.' The tragedy of all the misteaching that abounds today is that it leaves Christian with the same Old Covenant fear of God's displeasure if the Believer is disobedient. As it is the lot of every honest Believer to acknowledge that he or she is still disobedient, then it is quite common to find Christians who fear that, in some way, their disobedience – and God's reaction to that – is responsible for the hard times, or the 'desert experience' or the apparent lack of communion with God which the Believer may be experiencing.

That is not very good news because it puts the responsibility upon the Believer to 'get right with God' – which is something that, in truth, Jesus has already achieved for the Believer for all eternity.

The Good News is that under the New Covenant, the Bible declares, in John 1:16 that, 'From the fullness of His grace we have all received one blessing after another.' The blessings the Believer receives from God are not related in any way to the Believer's obedience, nor any other aspects of the Believer's life. The blessings, in keeping with the Covenant of Grace, are freely given to every Believer out of the abundance of God's grace.

In Romans 8:1 there is a well known verse which is so often quoted by Believers, yet equally often set aside in their relationship with God when the Believer becomes especially aware of sin in his or her life. The verse says, 'Therefore, there is now no condemnation for those who are in Christ Jesus.' The word 'No' must mean just that – there is NO condemnation for the Believer. That must obviously include those times when the Believer is disobedient, even when that disobedience is deliberate and repeated. This makes sense when it is remembered that obedience is not an obligation under the Covenant of Grace. It has already been established that the Believer is saved, justified, made righteous and sanctified by faith. It follows then that as long as faith remains there is nothing that can negatively affect the Believer's position or relationship with God.

In answer to the question, 'What are the consequences if a Christian is not obedient?' the answer is: There are no consequences as far as the Believer's relationship with God is concerned; but that Believer may be mastered by an unhelpful habit and may be a less effective witness.

Conclusion

Grace is not grace if it carries obligations, strings or conditions; therefore, obedience cannot be an obligation under the New Covenant.

The obedience primarily required by God is that man should believe in His Son Jesus Christ. A practical obedience then flows from this spiritual obedience.

Practical obedience is a responsibility which, if the Christian accepts the responsibility, is of benefit to the Christian and his fellow man, but in no way enhances or detracts from the Christian's relationship with God.

The Rule of Life for the Christian is Christ's law. It is a law which brings freedom, is rooted in love, is primarily concerned with the well-being of others and is not a heavy load.

The Christian is empowered to be obedient to Christ's law by the God-given gifts of faith, the Holy Spirit, grace, love and Jesus Christ. At no point is the Christian expected to be obedient in his own strength; but only through God's equipping.

In the event that the Christian, for whatever reason, chooses not to accept the responsibility to be practically obedient, that choice does not affect in any way the blessings that God will continue to pour out nor the relationship between the Christian and God. By being disobedient to Christ's law, the Christian risks being mastered by a sinful habit and becoming an ineffective witness. 'By the grace of God I am what I am, and His grace to me was not without effect. No, I worked harder than all of them – yet not I, but the grace of God that was with me' (1 Corinthians 15:10).

CHAPTER 10

Righteousness

Introduction
Jesus Christ said, '... My yoke is easy and My burden is light' (Matt. 11:30). For many Christians this Scripture is a nonsense because Christ's yoke appears very hard and His burden appears very heavy. There is no heavier burden that Christians carry than the burden of their own righteousness - their own right standing before God. The first purpose of this chapter is to show that a Christian's right standing before God is eternally achieved and assured by Jesus Christ. The second purpose of this chapter is to show where a Christian's lifestyle fits into his/her relationship with God.

The writer of Hebrews makes the point that it is possible to be in the faith for a long time and yet still be spiritually immature and unfruitful. In Hebrews 5:12 he says, 'In fact, though by this time you ought to be teachers, you need someone to teach you the elementary truths of God's Word all over again. You need milk, not solid food.' In the next verse the writer goes on to give the reason for this spiritual immaturity and lack of fruit. Hebrews 5:13 says, 'Anyone who lives on milk, being still an infant, is not acquainted with the teaching about righteousness.' The importance of understanding righteousness is that it will lead to spiritual maturity and will lead to fruit being produced in the life of the Christian.

The problem for many Christians is that their lack of understanding of the Scriptures' teaching on righteousness leads to a striving for righteousness - not understanding that it is God who brings it about. This lack of understanding is made worse by teaching that says a lack of righteousness in a Christian's life affects their standing before God.

There should be no doubt that God commands all Believers into right living; but there needs to be a clear understanding of how that is achieved. Equally, there needs to be a clear understanding of exactly how a Christian achieves right standing before God.

Lack of understanding of these matters, as the Bible itself teaches, leads to spiritual immaturity and lack of fruit. It leads to a seesaw relationship with God for the individual Believer, it leads to a sense of failure, heaviness, depression, condemnation and, eventually, can lead to Believers falling away completely from any attempt to live out their faith.

The Bible's teachings on righteousness

In relation to man, the Bible teaches that there are two types of righteousness. There is an internal righteousness and an external righteousness. Both Testaments of the Bible speak of these two types of righteousness for man.

The internal righteousness of the Old Testament comes through the Covenant of Abraham. The Bible says, 'Abram believed the Lord, and He credited it to him as righteousness' (Gen. 15:6). Abram (Abraham) had a righteousness of character, given to him by God. This righteousness was not a result of the way Abraham lived, but as a result of his faith in God. A look at the lifestyle of Abraham shows that, like all Believers, he continued to sin; but, the righteousness given to him, through his faith, was sufficient for salvation. Jesus, when challenging the Sadducees about their lack of faith in the resurrection, confirms the fact of Abraham's salvation in Matt. 22:32 when He quotes God as saying, 'I am the God of Abraham, the God of Isaac and the God of Jacob.' And Jesus goes on to say, 'He is not the God of the dead, but of the living.'

The external righteousness of man, as taught in the Old Testament came through the Covenant of Moses. It was an earned righteousness which was determined entirely by a person's lifestyle and could, therefore, vary from moment to moment. This righteousness was not given by God, it was through lifestyle not faith and, although it could give a certain right-standing before God, it was insufficient for salvation. Amongst many such Scriptures, Romans 3:20 makes clear, 'Therefore no-one will be declared righteous in His sight by observing the law; rather, through the law we become conscious of sin.'

The New Covenant in Christ's blood, as revealed through the New Testament, also speaks of this internal and external righteousness. As with the Covenant of Abraham, through the Covenant of Christ God freely gives an internal righteousness to man as a response to man's faith. The Covenant of Christ also teaches a right way of living that leads to an external righteousness. The gift of righteousness under the Covenant of Christ brings with it the gift of the Holy Spirit (Acts 2:38-39). It is the Holy Spirit who then works His righteousness from the inside outwards into right living for the Believer. Romans 8:11 says, 'And if the Spirit of Him who raised Jesus from the dead is living in you, He who raised Christ from the dead will also give life to your mortal bodies through His Spirit, who lives in you.'

When God commands the Believer into right living, He is telling the Believer to live the way He has recreated him/her in Christ. Living out a given righteousness is the command, not seeking to earn a right standing before God. Through inner righteousness to outward right living is the sequence. The Holy Spirit is the One who gives the first and brings about the second. That is what every Believer needs to understand about the Bible's teachings on righteousness.

The Christian inheritance

There are some very important verses in Galatians 3 which establish the position and, therefore, the inheritance of the Christian. The verses are Gal. 3:15-18. When these verses are understood then the question of the Believer's position before God, and how that position is achieved, is settled forever. Such understanding will bring peace to the striving Christian, hope to the struggling Christian, joy to the 'failing' Christian and, beyond the individual, it will bring unity within the church.

These verses, Gal. 3:15-18, say, 'Brothers, let me take an example from everyday life. Just as no-one can set aside or add to a human covenant which has been duly established, so it is in this case. The promises were spoken to Abraham and to his seed. The Scripture does not say, "and to seeds," meaning many people, but "and to your seed" meaning one person, who is Christ. What I mean is this: The law, introduced 430 years later, does not set aside the covenant previously established and thus do away with the promise. For if the inheritance depends upon the law, then it no longer depends on a promise; but God in His grace gave it to Abraham through a promise.' These verses start by pointing out that no-one can add to, take away from or set aside a duly established covenant. The whole point of a covenant was that it could not be altered in any way. These Scriptures go on to say that God established such an unalterable Covenant with Abraham – and with his seed. The basis of that relationship was a righteousness given through faith. The heir of this Covenant was not Abraham's natural descendants, it was not Israel; but was one person – Jesus Christ.

Gal. 3:29 then provides the link between the Abrahamic Covenant and the Christian. Gal. 3:29 says, 'If you belong to Christ, then you are Abraham's seed, and heirs according to the promise.' The Covenant was with Abraham, it was a covenant of faith; Christ was the sole heir to Abraham and to the promise. The Christian belongs to Christ, inherits all that is Christ's and, therefore, becomes heir to the Abrahamic covenant of faith. This is the sequence by which the Christian achieves his standing before God – his righteousness given by God in response to faith. The question may arise, 'If the Christian is heir to Abraham, what was the need for Christ?' Firstly, the Abrahamic Covenant was made with only two people – Abraham and Jesus. The Christian, therefore, cannot relate to God through Abraham. Christ's sacrifice was in order that the Christian, through faith in the shed blood, might be deemed by God to be 'in Christ' (Eph. 1:13) and, therefore, become an heir to the Abrahamic Covenant (Gal. 3:29). This is by no means a technical, theological point. Once understood, this will put an end to so much striving, so much doubt, so much confusion about a Christian's standing before, and relationship with, God. It is a foundation of the Christian faith. Secondly, Jesus Christ had to come and suffer in order that God's perfect justice may be satisfied. Although Abraham was given right-standing before God as a result of his faith, nevertheless someone still had to die for his sins – and the sins of those who would inherit through Abraham. Thus, the Christian is heir to two Covenants – that of Abraham and the New Covenant of Christ.

Gal. 3:17 goes on to address the issue of the Law of Moses – a subject which, particularly with the Ten Commandments, causes much confusion and consternation within Christian circles. Must Christians obey it? What is the effect on the Christian's relationship with God if the Christian does not seek to obey the Ten Commandments? Paul answers those questions, and many others, when he writes in Gal. 3:17, 'What I mean is this: The law, introduced 430 years later, does not set aside the covenant previously established by God and thus do away with the promise.' God, through Paul, is reassuring His people that the Law of Moses is a matter of total irrelevance to the Christian. In Romans 9:4 it says that the Law was given to Israel. Gal. 3:15 has already shown the impossibility of adding to a covenant. Gentile Believers are not Israel; the Law was not given to Gentiles – and that covenant cannot be altered. The Christian relates to God, as explained, through Christ and Abraham – and the separate Covenant of Moses has no bearing on the previously established covenant. When the Christian understands his inheritance, and how he comes into that inheritance, it will be seen that, in keeping with everything to do with the Covenant of Christ, it at no stage points the Christian to himself or his effort. The Gospel is all about what God has done, is doing and will do for man.

These few verses in Galatians establish clearly that the inheritance received by the Christian is righteousness from God, and before God, through faith. It is because of this God-given righteousness that Christians enter into an eternal relationship with God which begins at conversion and remains uninterrupted for all eternity.

The Pharisee and the tax collector (Luke 18:9-14)

The word for 'righteousness' in the New Testament/Covenant has two applications – one to character, the other to actions. These applications correspond to the inner righteousness of faith and the external righteousness of right living. Understanding the given, inner righteousness (character) which the Christian always has through faith will prevent the misapplication of Scriptures referring to righteousness in the New Testament.

This parable was told by Jesus to those 'who were confident of their own righteousness [external right living] and looked down on everyone else.' There are two important issues addressed in the reason for the telling of this parable. The first is that Jesus is making the point that no-one should ever feel confident of their own self-righteousness and, secondly, that such a self-confidence brings disunity – those who thought they were doing well looked down on the others. On the face of it, the Pharisee had reason to be self-confident. The Law demanded that a person fast once a week; this Pharisee fasted twice a week. The Law demanded a tithe of a tenth of all agricultural produce, this Pharisee gave a tenth of everything he had. Finally, the Pharisee appeared to be giving the credit to God with his opening statement, 'God, I thank *You* that I am not like other men . . .' (author's emphasis). On the other hand, the tax collector is aware of only two things – his sinfulness and God's mercy. Acknowledging the one and appealing to the other, he says only, 'God have mercy on me a sinner.' Jesus finishes the parable by informing His listeners that it is the tax collector who goes home justified. He is still a tax collector when he goes home. There is nothing in the Scriptures to say that his justification involved a change of livelihood. The important thing is that he went home a justified tax collector. His character, not his lifestyle, was deemed justified because of his faith. This is a very important point for all Believers. There are things in the lives of most Believers that should not be there. It could be something as dramatic, as in this parable, as the way the Believer earns his or her living. Or it may be less obvious matters, such as a pattern of thoughts or behaviour. The point here for all Believers is that these matters do not affect their right standing before God. The Believer's right standing before God is due, entirely, to the work that Christ has done on behalf of the Believer and the Believer's faith in that atoning work. Understanding that truth will bring a greater unity because it highlights the fact that the standing of each Believer before God is totally dependent upon the efforts of another – Christ. No-one, therefore, has any reason to look up to another Christian or, perhaps more importantly, look down upon another Christian.

Knowing this truth, of righteousness through faith, gives the Believer a confidence before God, as the Believer comes to God the Father with the eternal, unalterable right standing achieved for him by Jesus. With this knowledge there is no need for a seesaw relationship with God, no need for a sense of heaviness, failure or condemnation.

Knowing he is eternally righteous gives the Believer a boldness in his relationship with God which will, irrespective of the day's or week's events, allow him to 'approach the throne of grace with confidence, so that we may receive mercy and find grace to help us in our time of need' (Heb. 4:16).

The Christian is called into holy living and a lack of holy living may affect the Christian's ability to be an effective witness and so hinder the spread of the Gospel. For that, and other reasons, the Christian should always consider his way of life; but the Christian must never allow his way of life to become a barrier between him and God. It is when the Believer's lifestyle is falling short that the Believer is most in need of God's grace and mercy – which is why Hebrews 4:16 encourages the Believer to, at that time, draw close to the throne of God. Yet it is at that very time that many Believers draw back from God. That is why so many stay immature – they tend to cut themselves off from their source of help at the very time when it is most needed. The Christian's right living will be affected by his right standing because as the Believer comes into God's presence, with confidence, he receives according to Heb. 4:16 the help needed to bring about the change in lifestyle, which brings it more into line with the inner righteousness given by Christ – but it works from the inside out.

New Covenant teachings on righteousness

The reason for Christian immaturity, given in Hebrews 5:13, is lack of acquaintance with the teaching about righteousness. Some of the New Covenant teachings on righteousness follow. It is important, in order to understand these teachings, to use the correct application of the word 'righteousness.' Righteousness, in terms of 'right standing before God' is by faith, and faith alone.

Romans 1:17 says, 'For in the gospel a righteousness from God is revealed, a righteousness that is by faith from first to last.' Two very important truths about righteousness are revealed in this Scripture. First, the Believer's righteousness is FROM God. It flows from heaven to earth, from God to man. Secondly, it is a righteousness that comes through faith – entirely, completely by faith. Romans 3:21 reinforces the point of the God given nature of righteousness when it says, 'But now a righteousness FROM God, apart from the law, has been made known ...' (author's emphasis). Christian righteousness is from God and is unrelated to the way the Christian is living. **Romans 3:22** tells how this righteousness from God is given to the Believer. The verse says, 'This righteousness from God comes through faith in Jesus Christ to all who believe.' The righteousness that God gives is given as a response to faith in Jesus Christ and it is given to all who believe. So the struggling Christian, who may appear to be failing utterly to live the Christian life, is given the same right standing before God as the Believer who is living a much more obviously Christian life, because faith and not lifestyle is the issue. God is the originator of Christian righteousness and faith is the vehicle.

Romans 4:5 again makes the point that it is the Believer's faith which gives him right-standing before God; it says, 'However, to the man who does not work but trusts God who justifies the wicked, his faith is credited as righteousness.' It is reassuring to read that God justifies the wicked. The Good News is that such a truth, far from leading the Believer to abuse God's grace, is more likely to make the Believer fall in love with such a gracious God and, as Jesus promised His followers, 'If anyone loves Me, he will obey My teaching' (John 14:23). So faith, not works, leads to righteousness. **Romans 4:13** makes the link between the righteousness given to Abraham, because of his faith, and that inherited by his heir – which, as has been explained, means Jesus and then the Christian.

Romans 5:17 is one of those simple verses which, once seen and understood, can radically alter the Believer's relationship with

God. It says, '... how much more will those who receive God's abundant provision of grace and of the *GIFT* of righteousness reign in life through the one man, Jesus Christ' (author's emphasis). Righteousness is a GIFT! It is not earned, it is not contributed towards, it is not at risk of being taken away – it is a gift which, once given, belongs to the person receiving it. It is, as is any gift, free. The Believer's part in righteousness is not in striving, continual recommitment and greater effort; it is simply to receive righteousness as a gift from God. Understanding this one Scripture opens up the way to relieving the Believer of any sense of heaviness, striving, failure and so on. It opens up the way for the Believer to live in the joy of his or her salvation, secure in their standing, at all times, before God. This verse has enormous implications for the Believer. It says that if righteousness and grace are freely received then the Believer will 'reign in life.' Once again, great news for the struggling Christian. Great news for the Christian who thinks that God could never be pleased with them, for the Believer who thinks he will never overcome that old sinful pattern of thought or behaviour.

Romans 6:13 commands the Believer to 'not offer the parts of your body to sin' and goes on, in the same verse, to say, '... offer the parts of your body to Him as instruments of righteousness.' This refers to a righteousness of actions not of character and, therefore, does not affect the Christian's right standing with God. However such a command can heavily burden a Christian who may be offering the parts of their body to sin, particularly if that Christian cannot see a way whereby he or she can stop offering the parts of their body to sin, and so be obedient to God in this command. This, though, is a verse for the saved, not for the unsaved. Paul confirms this is the following verse, Romans 6:14, when he goes on to say to his readers, '... you are not under law, but under grace.' Such a statement can only be said of the saved and sealed Believer. When reading such a verse, and to avoid the burden of failure and condemnation, the Believer must go back to Romans 5:17 and see the way by which they may overcome any sinful habits – by receiving grace and the gift of righteousness. Let the reader go to Romans 6:14 and receive the confirmation that

'Sin shall not be your master... because you are under grace.' The Christian, with a full understanding of grace and righteousness need never fear the commands of God; but from the Word of God receive the hope that comes when the way of obedience is rightly grasped.

Romans 6:16 speaks of '... obedience, which leads to righteousness.' This is the sort of verse which leads people, Believers and unbelievers, to say that a Christian has to be obedient in order to become righteous. Such an understanding flies in the face of so many other Scriptures which speak of Christ as the righteousness of the Believer, of a righteousness that comes from God, of a righteousness which is by faith from beginning to end and of a righteousness which is a gift from God. The Christian is called, indeed commanded, into obedience; but not the shallow obedience which leads merely to an outer righteousness – that is, a show of right living. Christians are called '... to the obedience that comes from faith' (Rom. 1:5). Such an obedience will lead to a fulfilling of God's requirement of the Believer. Jesus was asked, 'What must we do to do the work God requires?' Jesus answered them, 'The work of God is this: to believe in the One He has sent.' (John 6:28-29). Belief in Jesus Christ meets God's requirement of man – that is the word of Jesus Himself – not an endless round of striving for external obedience to a set of rules and regulations.

Romans 8:10 shows the clear distinction between the outward battle with sin and the inner, undisturbed righteousness of the Christian. The verse says, 'But if Christ is in you, your body is dead because of sin, yet your spirit is alive because of righteousness.' Christ is in every Believer, so this verse, addressed to those who have Christ in them, is addressed to Believers. It is the spirit of the Believer which is righteous and alive, eternally, in and with Christ. The body, even of the Believer, is dead because of sin. No Christian should allow the daily activities of his/her body to separate him/her from spirit-strengthening communion with their Father. That communion is the Believer's as a right through faith (John 1:12); it is not earned as a result of lifestyle, so it is unaffected by daily living.

Romans 9:30-32 are important verses that teach the way of righteousness. Paul writes, 'What then shall we say? That the Gentiles, who did not pursue righteousness, have obtained it, a righteousness that is by faith; but Israel, who pursued a law of righteousness, has not attained it. Why not? Because they pursued it not by faith but as if it were by works.' It could not be more clearly stated. The Christian is righteous by faith, and not by works.

The sad reality today is that many Believers are still being taught that a Christian has to work for his righteousness. The way to be righteous before God is to believe in Jesus Christ and to receive, as a gift, righteousness from God. If Christians understood this it would make the Believers the bearers of truly Good News. Good News that would strengthen and encourage many a struggling Believer. Good News that would allow the wayward non-believer to dare to believe that God will accept, and love, even them. Good News that would increase the unity of Believers and, so, increase the effectiveness of Christian witness in the world. It should not be under-estimated just how important is a correct understanding of righteousness.

Romans 10:3 shows the danger of seeking to establish one's own righteousness – it can lead to a rejection of God's righteousness. 'Since they [Israel] did not know the righteousness that comes from God and sought to establish their own, they did not submit to God's righteousness.' The following verse, ***Romans 10:4***, states once again that '... there may be righteousness for everyone who believes.'

1 Corinthians 1:30 is a glorious verse which shows just how much Christian salvation, and righteousness, is a work of God for man. It starts by stating, 'It is because of Him that you are in Christ Jesus...'. Here is the Word of God declaring very simply that it is God's work that has brought the Believer into the position of being 'in Christ.' The verse goes on to say, '... you are in Christ Jesus, who has become for us wisdom from God – that is, our righteousness, holiness and redemption.' The wonderful news of the Gospel is that Christ Himself is the Christian's righteousness. It is Christ Himself who ensures the Christian's right standing before God, eternally. Jesus cannot be anything less that perfectly righteous and, so, because He is the righteousness of the Believer it means the Believer, likewise, can never be anything less than perfectly righteous in the sight of God. Such knowledge takes the burden of struggling away from the Believer. It allows the Believer to live in 'the joy of his salvation.' It empowers the Believer to be a channel of encouragement. It also, according to Romans 5:17, will lead the Believer to 'reign in life.'

Paul writes, in **Galatians 2:21**, 'I do not set aside the grace of God, for if righteousness could be gained through the law, Christ died for nothing.' God-given righteousness is an outworking of God's grace. Grace, in all its aspects, has to be free and unconditional – that is what makes it grace. Righteousness before God, therefore, has to be free and unconditional. It is foolishness to think that a Believer's daily living can add to, or take away from, the God-given gift of righteousness – which is Jesus Christ Himself. Let every Believer rejoice in his God-given righteousness and give thanks and glory to God for such a wonderful gift. As in all things in the Christian's relationship with God, let the Believer look to what God has done for him and not what he, the Believer, should be doing for God. That is the direction of Scripture.

In **Philippians 3:9** Paul states that he wants to 'be found in Him [Jesus], not having a righteousness of my own that comes from the law, but that which is through faith in Christ – the righteousness which comes from God and is by faith.' Paul had earlier declared, in Philippians 3:6, that with regard to 'legalistic righteousness' he was 'faultless.' So Paul was not a man who was seeking an easy option in order to avoid the need for obedience. Paul excelled in his observance of the Law of Moses; but he came to realise that, despite all his efforts to live right, he had not achieved right-standing with God. Paul came to understand that such a right-standing must be a gift from God, through Jesus.

There are Scriptures which appear to encourage the Believer to strive for his own righteousness. Paul writes to Timothy, in 1 Timothy 6:11, 'But you, man of God, flee from all this, and pursue righteousness . . .' Believers need not be afraid of or confused by, such Scriptures. As has been written earlier in this chapter, there are two applications of the word righteous in the New Testament –

one referring to character and the other referring to actions. Righteousness of character, as so many Scriptures have shown, is a gift from God which comes through faith. Clearly Paul is not encouraging Timothy to pursue righteousness of character – indeed, he refers to Timothy, in the same verse, as a 'man of God.' Paul in this and other such Scriptures, is clearly encouraging his young disciple to pursue a righteousness of actions which will demonstrate his righteousness of character. The Scriptures do teach that sin is no longer an issue between God and man; however, the Scriptures do not encourage the Believer to adopt a casual attitude towards sin. In this verse Paul is simply encouraging Timothy to adopt a firm attitude towards any wrong living in his life. The same understanding applies to 2 Timothy 2:22 where Paul, once again, encourages Timothy to live out his God-given righteousness.

God has made the Believer righteous, so God encourages Believers to live righteously. He is simply calling the Believer to be what God has made him. The problems come when Believers try to be something beyond what God has called them to be. The Believer must live in the freedom he has, must live in the authority he has been given and must pursue right living; but, at no stage, must a Believer allow lifestyle to separate him from fellowship with God.

Conclusion

Right standing before God is by faith. Right living, or lack of right living, does not affect the Believer's right standing. Understanding the Scriptures' teachings on righteousness will:
(i) bring increased unity within the church – The Pharisee and the Tax Collector;
(ii) increase fruit bearing – Col. 1:6 and other verses;
(iii) bring increased spiritual maturity – Hebrews 5:13;
(iv) bring a boldness and confidence in the Believer's relationship with God – Heb. 4:16;
(v) put Christ at the very centre of the Believer's relationship with God – Rom. 5:1.

For the very important reasons listed above, understanding

RIGHTEOUSNESS

righteousness is vital for the Believer. A lack of understanding will have a crippling effect upon the individual Believer and upon the Church overall. The Christian's God-given gift of eternal, unalterable, righteousness through Christ is at the very heart of the Christian Gospel – and that's Good News!

PART THREE – **MORE GOOD NEWS**

CHAPTER 11

Some very ordinary people

Introduction
Many Christians, indeed probably all Christians, start out on their Christian life with every intention of living the kind of life that will be pleasing to God, will be a real witness to those around them, will encourage their brothers and sisters in the faith and will lead many non-believers into a living faith in Christ Jesus. The experience of many, if not most Christians, is that it is impossible to live up to those high standards – standards which have their roots in Scripture and can all be supported by verses from the Bible. The Christian has now slipped, at least in his or her own eyes, and believes themselves to be failing God, letting Him down by being a poor witness. The Christian in this position of realising their human frailty, perhaps being disappointed in their lack of commitment and despondent about ever changing, is faced with three choices. Firstly, the Christian can set about striving to be a different person. Making lots more effort to overcome old habits; setting their will firmly behind following Jesus, no matter the cost. Secondly, the Christian can simply give up. This can manifest in varying degrees. It may mean sitting in the back pews of the church, going through the motions but, essentially, contributing nothing to the advancement of the Kingdom – through perceived inadequacy rather than through lack of desire. At its extreme, the following of this choice can mean a complete severing of all links with the Christian church, stopping all Christian activity such as Bible reading, prayer and worship in the privacy of one's own home and even the cutting off of

Christian friendships on the basis of no longer having anything in common.

The third choice is to receive more of God's grace, even whilst in the midst of sin and failure and, like Paul in Philippians 3:14, to '... press on towards the goal ...'

Sadly, too many Christians are choosing one of the first two choices listed - mainly because they are unaware of the third choice. Scriptures teach that the third choice is the correct choice - that by receiving more of God's grace the changes will come. This chapter looks at various people through the Scriptures who have started out with every good intention of serving God, have plumbed the depths of experiencing failure in all its many facets and yet, by receiving grace, have gone on to serve God despite their human frailty. This chapter is an exercise in encouragement in which a brief look will be taken at some of the 'Greats' of the Christian faith. This look will reveal that, like all Christians today, these so-called 'Greats' were in reality very ordinary human beings, full of human frailty. It was for them, as it is for the Christian today, God's grace which made, and makes, the difference. This chapter will reveal that the 'Greats' of the Christian faith knew what it was to live in fear of man, to struggle with lust, to descend to suicidal despair, to doubt God, to be a bad parent, to commit murder, to be disobedient, to dishonour God, to struggle with inadequacy, to commit idolatry, to give in to favouritism, to commit adultery, to struggle with anger and to have lack of faith. The men and women who exhibited these glaring examples of human frailty are some of the same men and women who are listed in Hebrews chapter 11 - which lists those who are renowned for their faith. The glory of God is that He uses very ordinary, very frail people with such obvious faults. The joy of the Christian today is the Biblical promise that God never changes and that today God still uses very ordinary, very frail people with very obvious faults. The point of this chapter is not to bring down the 'Greats' of the Christian faith by highlighting their failings; the point is to exalt a God who, by His grace, raises up ordinary people to the position of being great in Him.

In the beginning . . .

In Genesis chapter 1 is the story of creation. In verse 27 it tells of how God created man in His own image and in verse 31, as God surveys His creation, He sees that it is 'very good.' At this point Adam and Eve are doing well in their relationship with God. Yet despite everything that God had done, and provided, for him, it wasn't long before Adam failed to live up to God's requirement. In Genesis chapter 3, verse 6, both Adam and Eve sinned by eating the fruit from the tree of the knowledge of good and evil, despite God's command not to do so. At this stage they enter into a sense of failure in their relationship with God. This is witnessed to by their own reaction – self-rejection (Gen. 3:7) and fear of God (Gen. 3:10). Adam and Eve choose the option of self-improvement. They attempt, as many Christians today, to change their situation through their own efforts (Gen. 3:7). Obviously their own efforts bring no peace with God, or real peace with each other, so when God approaches they hide from Him. God, at this point, takes over the problem and graciously provides them both with an adequate covering for their nakedness (Gen. 3:21). When this happens – through God's efforts on their behalf, through God's grace – they are enabled to cope with the reality of themselves and go on to follow God's direction for their lives. They were faced with a problem of their own making, a problem which was beyond them to resolve, so God resolved it for them. In Adam and Eve there is the illustration of God's dealing with mankind since creation. Man creates problems, man cannot solve those problems, God resolves them. The story starts with Adam and Eve, peaks at the cross of Christ and is equally, and powerfully, applicable for every Christian today.

The giving of the Law

Moses was chosen by God to have face to face fellowship with God. Moses is described in the Bible as being, 'more humble than anyone else . . . on earth' (Numbers 12:3). In Exodus 32:15, having been given the Law through which Israel would relate to God – and which was given to reveal the need for Jesus (Gal. 3:24) – Moses set off down the mountain to inform and instruct Israel.

While Moses was on the mountain Israel had lapsed into idolatrous worship of a golden calf. Moses, on learning of this idolatry, became very angry and smashed the tablets containing the recently given Law. This might sound a quite reasonable outburst of righteous anger, yet it is reasonable to assume from God's reaction to the broken tablets that it was not an action inspired by the Lord. So Moses, as the only human being entrusted with receiving the Law from God, had smashed to bits the only written record of that Law. God's reaction, in Exodus 34:1, is to provide Moses with a replacement set of tablets. Moses had a heart for God. He offered, following this incident of idol worship, to be 'blotted out of the book You have written' as a type of atonement for Israel. Yet, despite this heart inclined towards God, and despite the mighty way in which God revealed Himself to Moses, here and elsewhere Moses demonstrated his human frailty. It was Moses who having started so well - being entrusted with the Law - made a significant error, and it was God who sorted out the mistake for Moses.

Time and time again, as seen in this sequence of events, God sorts out the problems that man creates for himself - and God does so without any word of rebuke or rejection. This should be a source of great encouragement to all Christians - that God is big enough, and loving enough, to deal with all human frailty. In another incident Moses, in God's words, '. . . did not uphold My holiness among the Israelites' (Deut. 32:51); but despite that, God continued to use and bless Moses and allowed him to lead Israel right up to the edge of the Promised Land.

Abraham

Abraham was known as a man of faith. In Romans 4:18 it says that 'Against all hope, Abraham in hope believed and so became the father of many nations . . .' Abraham was called God's friend (2 Chron. 20:7) long before there was any concept that a man could actually be a friend to God. Yet despite the great faith for which Abraham is renowned, when God told Abraham that he and Sarah would have a child (Genesis 17:17) Abraham laughed at the idea of a man of nearly a hundred years old having a child and at the idea of Sarah, at ninety years old, having a child. It seemed so unlikely an idea to Abraham that he asked that God bless Ishmael, the child Abraham had fathered through Sarah's servant Hagar. The glory of God is that although He obviously knew of Abraham's doubt, yet He responded to Abraham's confidence in their relationship and agreed to Abraham's request that God bless Ishmael (Genesis 17:18). God, also, graciously fulfilled His word despite Abraham and Sarah's doubt and Isaac was duly born.

Abraham also suffered greatly from fear of men. Abraham on two occasions feared so much for his safety that he was prepared to allow other men to take Sarah as their wife (Gen. 12:13, Gen. 20:2). This was a man who had seen the angel of the Lord face to face, and yet feared for his life at the hands of men. On each occasion of Abraham's very human frailty God was still willing and able to use and bless Abraham. This roller-coaster of faith and doubt, confidence and fear is a reflection of the kind of turmoil that can afflict many Christians. What an encouragement for Christians today to see that those held up as the 'Greats' of the faith were, in reality, of the same frail material as all human beings – and that it was, and is, the grace of God that enabled them to achieve what they did achieve for God. Such knowledge allows the Christian today to accept his or her own weaknesses, and still have faith that he or she is of use within the Kingdom and will not be set aside as having nothing to contribute. God uses Christians today despite their weaknesses, not because of their strengths – as the Apostle Paul writes in 2 Corinthians 13:4, 'Likewise, we are weak in Him, yet by God's power we will live with Him to serve you.' It is by God's power.

Gideon

Gideon suffered from three common Christian experiences – doubt, a sense of inadequacy and fear of man. The story of Gideon is told in Judges chapters 6 and 7. Gideon started off from a very privileged position – he was actually sought out by the angel of the Lord. Gideon at that time was hiding from the Midianites who were oppressing Israel. The angel greeted Gideon as '... mighty warrior' (6:12) and assured Gideon that the Lord was with him. Gideon's immediate reaction was to question (6:13) what the angel had said because of the oppression being suffered by Israel. The angel informed Gideon that he, Gideon, was God's chosen instrument to free Israel from the Midianite oppression. Gideon's second reaction to God's call was a sense of inadequacy (6:15), protesting to the angel that he, Gideon, was the least qualified in all Israel to be its deliverer. Despite further reassurances, Gideon still struggled to believe what was being said and he asked the angel for a sign (6:17). The sign was duly given. Gideon finally set out to obey the Lord; but, racked by fear of man, he did so under cover of darkness (6:27). Following this provocation, the Midianites took up arms against Israel. Gideon began to summon a great army to fight Midian and, still doubting his calling and equipping by God, he asked Him for the two well-known signs involving the laying of a fleece (6:36-40). God graciously granted both signs. Gideon was still looking to man's strength instead of God's and gathered a great army to fight the Midianites. God had to gently remove the army, without a word of rebuke, and bring Gideon back to a point of being dependent upon Himself (7:2-6). On the night of the battle God again met with Gideon in the midst of his fear, and offered him yet another sign in order to convince Gideon that God really was going to use him (7:10-14). Gideon then went on and achieved God's purpose.

This is a story to wonderfully encourage even the most faint-hearted amongst modern Christians. Here was a man sought out by God, given three signs at his request, given a fourth sign by God; a man racked by fear of men, filled with doubt and a sense of inadequacy and yet mightily used by God. Throughout this story of doubt, fear and presumed inadequacy there is not one word of rebuke from God to Gideon. God takes the Believer and uses him exactly as he or she is and, in that way, the glory goes to God. Throughout these events Gideon received from God only understanding, encouragement, patience and reassurance. What God truly thought of Gideon can be seen by his inclusion in the list, in Hebrews 11, of the 'Greats' of the Christian faith. In Gideon, even if in no-one else, there is hope and inspiration for every Christian to, as Gideon himself was instructed, 'Go in the strength you have . . .'

Samson

Samson was in a very privileged position, yet he struggled with a problem which any Christian having the same battle would be very reluctant to acknowledge. Samson's problem was lust. Set aside for God before he was even born (Judges 13:4-5), his parents received divine guidance (13:13) on how to raise this child who was to be a Nazarite from birth. Samson, despite his blessed and privileged start in life, was made of frail human flesh. When he became a young man he was attracted to a young Philistine woman. It was God's instructions to Israel that they should not marry into the uncircumcised nations around them. Samson's parents reminded him of this, but he rejected their authority – something which could be punishable by death. The marriage to the Philistine woman proved a disaster and led to death and carnage all round (14:19 – 15:11). Samson next got involved with a prostitute (16:1-3). Following on from that, Samson fell in love with another Philistine woman, Delilah. Having already disobeyed God's rules regarding inter-marrying with non-Israelites, having been tricked by that first wife (14:17) and having seen carnage develop as a result of that trickery, Samson then repeated his folly. He married Delilah and was tricked once again. He revealed the secret of his strength and was taken captive by the Philistines. God's purpose for Samson had been to free Israel from Philistine oppression and, despite all the mistakes and wilful sinning of Samson, God never set him aside or gave up on Samson. Right at the end, captive and blind, Samson had the confidence in his relationship with God to call out to Him one more time (16:28). God graciously heard Samson's cry and answered it and Samson, in his final act as God's instrument against the oppressing Philistines, '. . . killed many more when he died than while he lived' (16:30). This is a story of a man with an essentially weak character, a man who obviously struggled with very human weaknesses including lust, and yet who was strong in God and was remembered by God. Another testimony, not to man's achievements for God, but of God's grace towards sinning men and women and of His achievements through such men and women.

Samuel
Samuel was set aside for God before his birth (1 Samuel 1:11). He ministered before God even before he knew God or could recognize His voice (1 Sam. 3:7). God greatly used Samuel throughout his whole life, but Samuel had one fault – he was a bad parent! That may not sound such a dramatic problem as those experienced by others in this chapter or, indeed, those experienced by Christians today; but the Scriptures reveal that this one fault was to have dire effects upon the whole nation of Israel. Samuel may have been able to lead Israel, but he was unable to lead his own family, and that is a situation in which many Christians might find themselves today. It is a source of encouragement that God is still willing and able to use such people. As Samuel grew older he appointed his sons as Judges over Israel (1 Sam. 8:1). He did this despite seeing what had happened to the previous High Priest and Judge, Eli, who also indulged his wayward sons and was rebuked by God for so doing (1 Sam. 2:29). Samuel did this despite the fact that the waywardness of his sons was well known throughout Israel. That waywardness was no minor matter. The Scriptures state that, 'They turned aside after dishonest gain and accepted bribes and perverted justice' (1 Sam. 8:3). Samuel appears, at this point, to have shown favouritism in contravention of the Law (Lev. 19:15) and to have ignored the rebellion of his sons – an offence punishable by stoning (Deut. 21:18-21). The result of this bad parenting, favouritism and indulgence is that the elders of Israel rejected Samuel's sons as Judges of Israel and demanded a king – as the other nations. Until that point God had been the King of Israel, so to demand a king was effectively for Israel to reject God and that rejection was confirmed by God when He said to Samuel, '... it is not you they have rejected as their king, but Me' (1 Sam. 8:7). Although Samuel's bad parenting, favouritism and ignoring of the Law of Moses contributed towards, and was even indirectly responsible for, Israel rejecting God, yet God did not reject Samuel. God subsequently used Samuel to anoint Saul as the first King of Israel and, later, to seek out and anoint David as Saul's successor. Once again, here is a story in which, despite some very obvious

failures and weaknesses, there is no rebuke from God to Samuel. So even though the sin of a Christian today may cause others to stumble, or even fall, the witness of Scripture is that such an event does not render that Christian without use within the Kingdom of God.

David

This is the story (1 Samuel 16 onwards) of a man greatly blessed by God, flawed by human frailty and yet graciously dealt with and further used for God's purposes. David, the youngest of eight sons, was sought out and anointed as the future King of Israel by the prophet and priest Samuel while he, David, was still effectively a boy. The Lord protected and blessed David throughout his life – from the lion and the bear (1 Sam. 17:37), from the sword of Goliath (1 Sam. 17:46) and from all his enemies (1 Sam. 20:15). David was used by God to defeat the enemies of Israel and was considered by God to be, '... a man after My own heart ...' (Acts 13:22). God made David King over Israel and gave him victory, wealth and honour.

David was a man who was very committed to following and obeying God – as may be said of many Christians today. Yet like so many of those Christians today, David fell victim to the human frailty which is evident in all human being, albeit in different forms. In 2 Samuel 11 is the story of David's adultery with Bathsheba and his arranging for the murder of her husband, Uriah the Hittite. Murder and adultery are probably beyond the range of most Christians who feel they are failing God, yet, even in the light of such obvious sins, God did not reject David nor set him aside. God continued to use David and to bless him and, ultimately, to make the son of David and Bathsheba, Solomon, the next King of Israel.

These examples should not be taken to mean that the Scriptures portray God as soft on sin. The Bible states quite clearly that God 'hates' sin. The Bible also states quite clearly that 'Where sin increased, grace increased all the more ...' (Romans 5:20). These stories testify not to a soft attitude to sin, but to a grace that is big enough to overcome even the greatest sin. In that lies the hope of every Christian who would seek to serve and follow God. The ultimate accolade shown to David, which is an astounding witness to God's acceptance of frail and even wilful sinners, is that Jesus Christ, the Son of God, is also known, in fulfilment of prophecy, as the Son of David. No Christian need ever fear that God will reject them because it is His grace, and not their lifestyle, that keeps them secure.

Solomon

The story of Solomon is in 1 Kings, from chapter 1 through to chapter 11. Although he was known as the wisest man on earth (1 Kings 4:31), Solomon still had to rely upon the grace of God. The Scriptures pay compliment to Solomon at the start of his reign as King of Israel. In 1 Kings 3:3 it states that, 'Solomon showed his love for the Lord by walking according to the statutes of his father David, except that he offered sacrifices and burned incense on the high places.' These were the very 'high places' that God had ordered Israel to destroy in Numbers 33:52. These high places were sites of Canaanite worship and were sites of idolatrous worship and sacrifice, they were sites of immorality and often had shrine prostitutes present. Israel had been ordered by God to destroy them, but had disobeyed. Solomon visited what is described, in 1 Kings 3:4, as the 'most important high place.' There he offered a thousand burnt offerings to the Lord. Solomon slept that night at that 'most important high place' after a day of offering burnt offerings and incense, and it was there that God chose to meet with him in a dream and extend His grace towards Solomon. God does not rebuke Solomon for failing to destroy the high place, but amazingly says to him, 'Ask Me for whatever you want Me to give you' (1 Kings 3:4). It was at that point that God granted to Solomon the wisdom for which he is renowned and, God said, 'I will give you . . . riches and honour – so that in your lifetime you will have no equal amongst kings' (1 Kings 3:13). The power of God's grace to transform people is illustrated wonderfully in this story about Solomon. Shown grace, even at the site of 'the most important high place,' Solomon's immediate reaction to God's mercy was to return to Jerusalem and offer sacrifices to God before the Ark of the Covenant. Receiving grace, and this is the point of this chapter, brings about the kind of lifestyle that many Christians spend so long striving to achieve in their own strength.

Elijah

In 1 Kings 18 is the inspiring story of Elijah's duel with the false prophets of Baal. At Mount Carmel Elijah faced 450 of Baal's prophets in a contest to show Israel who was the true God. Elijah demonstrated great courage and faith as he, through the power of God, humiliated the prophets of Baal, had them executed and then declared the end of a drought that had been severely afflicting Israel. As the rain approached, Elijah advised the king, Ahab, to hitch up his chariot and race ahead of the oncoming rain back to the town of Jezreel. Ahab followed that advice, whilst Elijah proceeded to run on foot all the way to Jezreel ahead of Ahab's chariot. Immediately after that amazing sequence of events, Elijah fell victim to his own humanity, and fear overtook him completely. When Elijah heard that the queen, Jezebel, planned to kill him he was consumed with fear and fled to the desert (1 Kings 19). There then unfolds a wonderful revelation of God's grace and how He deals with His people. Elijah had reached a point of total despair. He actually prayed that he would die. He had given in completely to despair, fear and depression. Exhausted, and emotionally drained, he fell asleep. God sent an angel to minister to Elijah and he was awoken by the angel to find newly baked bread and a jar of water prepared for him. There was no word of rebuke from God to Elijah, there was no comment at all upon the situation; God simply meets Elijah's immediate physical needs. After more rest, and a second visit from the angel with food and drink, Elijah was sufficiently refreshed to travel to the mountain of Horeb. At Horeb God met with Elijah and began to meet his spiritual needs. It started with a simple question, put in such a way that Elijah was confident enough to be honest with God about how he felt and how he saw the situation (1 Kings 19:10). God then revealed His presence to Elijah. Again the question came, 'What are you doing here Elijah?' (1 Kings 19:13) and Elijah gave the same answer as before. God then further commissioned Elijah to go immediately and anoint two future kings and a future prophet. Despite the circumstances in which God had met Elijah, He had the confidence to give him these tasks. God does not lay people aside simply because of their weaknesses. God's confidence was not in Elijah, and is not in the Christian of today; God's confidence is in Himself to achieve His purposes through His chosen instrument – whether that instrument is Elijah, Gideon, Samson or a modern day, equally frail and fickle, Christian.

Peter

Peter is a wonderful example for every Christian who seeks to enthusiastically follow Jesus, even in the midst of their own weaknesses and frailty. An example of Peter's desires to follow Jesus is given in Matthew chapter 14. It is the story of Jesus walking on the water of the lake. Peter demonstrated his faith in Jesus by climbing over the side of the boat, despite the fierce wind, and himself walking on water. Peter then took his eyes off Jesus and, noticing the high wind, his faith failed, was replaced by fear and he began to sink. Many a Christian has set out to serve and follow Jesus and been distracted, even discouraged, by the circumstances. The important point is not the actions of Peter, but the reaction of Jesus. As soon as Peter called to Jesus for help, Jesus put out His hand and rescued Peter. Jesus at no point asked more from Peter than he was able to give. When Peter reached the end of his faith, Jesus took over.

Another example of God's grace to His people, from the life of Peter, concerns how Peter in Matthew 26:35 declared that even if all the other disciples deserted Jesus, he, Peter, was ready to die with Jesus. Later, when fear for his own life overcame him, Peter did – despite his heartfelt good intentions – deny Jesus. Again, there are many Christian who go through a similar experience. Their heart says one thing, but when the crunch comes they fail. Once again, the action of Peter, or the modern day Christian, is not the important point. What counts is the reaction of Jesus. The reaction of Jesus with Peter was to reinstate him (John 21:15-19). Jesus then allowed Peter the privilege of being the one to first announce the Gospel to the Jews and, later, to the Gentiles. The reaction of Jesus to the struggling Christian today is exactly the same. Jesus builds up, affirms, blesses and uses His people without regard to any supposed strengths or known weaknesses.

Mary Magdelene

As a devoted follower of Jesus, it is Mary, who, when the men are hiding in a locked room following Christ's crucifixion, goes to the tomb with spices for the body (Luke 24:1). It does not occur to her that Jesus may be alive, she goes with spices to care for His dead body. Although she believed Him to be dead, yet Mary was still prepared to publicly be associated with Jesus – even though the men were hiding for fear that such an association would cost them their lives. It was a courageous act, but one which, in truth, lacked any faith in, or understanding of, the resurrection. Jesus met with Mary and, with His customary lack of rebuke, revealed Himself to her as the Risen Christ. Mary, who had come with courage but no faith, returned to the disciples and was allowed the honour of being the first person to announce the resurrection (John 20:18). This is another example of how Jesus meets every Believer exactly at their point of need. Mary desired to serve Jesus even though she had no faith; Jesus met with her, gave her the faith and allowed her to serve Him by announcing His resurrection. It was Christ's grace that enabled Mary to serve her Lord.

Peter and John

When Mary reported that she had seen the Lord Jesus, Peter and John raced to the tomb. Peter was a little unsure of what had happened but John believed (John 20:8). Despite that, the men returned to the room in which they were hiding before Mary's announcement of the resurrection. Later Jesus appeared to the men in the locked room and, with no word of rebuke for their fear, reassured them and blessed them with His peace (John 20:19-21). This is an encouragement for any Christian who, despite knowing the truth, through fear of men – or any other reason – chooses to keep that truth hidden away. It is Good News that Jesus will not rebuke such a fearful Christian, but will bless them and grant them peace. Having received Christ's blessing and peace, Peter and John went on in time to become mighty evangelists for the Gospel. God takes each person exactly as they are and works with the person just as they are.

Thomas

In John chapter 11 Jesus was returning to hostile Judea in order to raise Lazarus from the dead. His disciples tried to talk Him out of the planned trip – reminding Him that during His last time there the Jews had tried to stone Him. Jesus, though, was determined to go and Thomas said to the rest of the disciples, 'Let us also go, that we may die with Him.' Here was a man who has passed into history as 'Doubting Thomas' and yet equally deserves the title, 'Heroic Thomas.' This is the position many Christians would like to occupy. The reality for every Christian, and the reality for Thomas, is that every person is a complex mix of weak and strong, good and bad, brave and cowardly and every other emotion and counter-emotion imaginable. It was the same Heroic Thomas who, when informed of Christ's resurrection, flatly refused to believe and declared he would not believe until he saw, and touched, the wounds of Christ. A week later Jesus appeared to the disciples, still within a locked room. Thomas was present and Jesus invited him to touch His wounds, and so believe. The humility of Christ shines through this encounter. His willingness to meet each person in the midst of their weakness is made abundantly clear by His reaction to Thomas. The extension of grace, and the receiving of it by Thomas, enabled Thomas to be the first to proclaim Jesus as God.

Conclusion

Time and time again, throughout the Scriptures, there are examples of men and women who have set out, with a good heart, to serve God. Again and again they have fallen victim to human frailty and weakness. The Scriptures show that God has a consistently gracious way of dealing with His people in the midst of their weaknesses. Christians should be encouraged by the stories of people like those given in this chapter, most of whom are regarded as the 'Greats' of the Christian faith. Like those whose stories have been told here, and countless others throughout Scripture and throughout history, Christians today who are struggling with fear of man, doubt, anger, bad parenting, lust, a sense of inadequacy, suicidal despair, adultery, even idolatry or murder or any other sin known to man should heed the lessons of the 'Greats', should receive more grace from God, should draw even closer to God and should serve, '... with the strength God provides...' (1 Peter 4:11). No greater striving, no giving up; simply a greater dependence upon His amazing grace.

CHAPTER 12

The Believer in Christ

Introduction
Throughout this book many doctrinal truths have been examined. Some who read this book will have problems accepting some of what has been written. Much has been written about grace and, again, some will have problems accepting grace in its entirety. When, however, a Christian reads through the Scriptures and discovers what God's Word says about the Believer, then that must be accepted – for it is written in the Bible in very clear terms and, as such, is not a matter for debate. There are many issues which the Christian may not understand, but the Believer can understand 'Who we are in Christ' – perhaps leaving the 'whys and wherefores' to the more theologically inclined. It is important that each Believer understands how God sees every Christian – even if the Christian doesn't grasp why God sees him or her in that way. It is in understanding what the Word says on such matters that the Believer will come to see him or herself as God sees them, and then there is a new confidence in their relationship with God, a new zeal, a new joy, a lightness of spirit and a new source of empowerment – love.

The *Good* News – Who the Believer is 'in Christ'
Throughout the New Testament, the position referred to for Believers is that they are 'in Christ.' The Bible speaks of how God sees the Believers as having '. . . clothed yourselves with Christ' (Gal. 3:27). It is because of this position, and this Divine clothing, that God is able to see the Christian in a way which does not necessarily relate to their own daily experience. Let every Christian know then that because of Jesus, all Believers:

can approach God with freedom and confidence	Eph. 3:12
are alive to God	Rom. 6:11

THE BELIEVER IN CHRIST

are brought near to God	Eph. 2:13
are called to eternal glory	1 Pet. 5:10
are justified	Gal. 2:17
are made alive	1 Cor. 15:22
are made equal with all other Believers	Gal. 3:20
are new creations	2 Cor. 5:17
are perfect	Col. 1:28
are reconciled to God	2 Cor. 5:19; Eph. 2:13
are resurrected	Acts 4:2
are sanctified	1 Cor. 1:2
are seated in the heavenly realms	Eph. 2:6
are set free to love	Gal. 5:6
are triumphant	2 Cor. 2:14
are united with all other Believers	Rom. 12:5
can pray continually	1 Thess. 5:17
do good works	Eph. 2:10
discover spiritual reality	Col. 2:17
experience joy	Phil. 1:26; 1 Thess. 5:16
fulfil God's plan	1 Cor. 1:30
have all their needs met	Phil. 4:19
have every good thing	Philem. 1:6
have forgiveness of sins	Col. 1:13-14
have freedom	Gal. 2:4
have received eternal life	Rom 5:21; Rom. 6:23
know peace of heart and mind	Phil. 4:7
know thankfulness	1 Thess. 5:18
live a new life	1 Cor. 4:17; 2 Tim. 1:1
receive every spiritual blessing	Eph. 1:3
receive God's forgiveness	Eph. 4:32
receive God's kindness and riches	Eph. 2:7
receive God's promise	2 Cor. 1:20
receive grace	1 Cor. 1:4; 2 Tim. 1:9; 2 Tim. 2:1
are set free from condemnation	Rom. 8:1
receive salvation	2 Tim. 2:10
receive the love of God	Rom. 8:39
stand firm	2 Cor. 1:21
understand God's truth	2 Cor. 3:14

All these Scriptures are true for the Believer because of the position the Believer has been given by God. Through faith the Believer has been placed 'in Christ.' God the Father, therefore, relates to every Believer in the same way in which He relates to Jesus (John 17:26). A giant step forward for every Christian is to learn to see themselves as God sees them. For example, the Believer may see himself as always failing in one particular area of his life, some sinful habit or thought pattern, and this may rob that Believer of some of the joy and confidence which he should be experiencing in his relationship with God. It is, therefore, liberating to know that God does not see the Believer as a failure; on the contrary, in Christ the Believer is seen by God as triumphant (2 Cor. 2:14). It is in grasping these truths, by faith, that a truly transforming way of thinking is obtained (Rom. 12:2). The list given is by no means exhaustive. Discovering such exciting truths makes Bible reading a pleasure, rather than just the Christian duty that it can so often become. When the Scriptures are read from the point of view of a Believer who is 'in Christ' then such reading is more likely to become the devotion that it was for the early church (Acts 2:42).

More *Good* News – What Jesus has achieved for the Believer

The essence of the Gospel story is that it is about what God, through Jesus, was doing, is doing and will continue to do for the Believer. Listed here are some of Christ's achievements for the Believer. Through Jesus, Believers:

offer sacrifices acceptable to God	1 Pet. 2:5
are adopted as sons of God	Eph. 5:1
are given the victory	1 Cor. 15:57
become pleasing to God	Heb. 13:21
bring praise to God	1 Pet. 4:11
are filled with the fruit of righteousness	Phil. 1:11
have peace with God	Acts 10:36; Rom. 5:1
are reconciled to God	Rom. 5:11
receive salvation	1 Thess. 5:9
receive the Holy Spirit	Titus 3:5-6

All these blessings, benefits and achievements belong to the Believer because of Jesus. They do not belong to the Believer because of any contribution whatsoever by the Believer. If any of these blessings are not being experienced it will be because the Believer is relating to God through his or her own achievement. For example, the Believer may feel that God is not very pleased with them because of something they are, or are not, doing. Yet the Bible says that - because of Jesus - Believers have become pleasing to God (Heb. 13:21). The important point for every Believer to grasp is that all that Christians are in the sight of God, they are because of Jesus. The blessings, benefits and achievements listed belong to every Believer because of what Jesus has done, who Jesus is and because of who the Believer is 'in Christ'. These benefits and blessings are all gifts from God to His people - unearned, undeserved, unconditional and unlimited. Living in the achievement of Christ will inevitably lead, as the Bible teaches (Col. 2:7), to a life that is overflowing with thankfulness.

Even more *Good* News – How God sees the Believer

The leap of faith necessary to really live in the fullness of Christ's achievement is for the Believer to see him or herself as God sees them. The following give some idea of how God sees the Believer. Regardless of the day to day ups and downs of a Believer's life and walk, God sees Believers as:

brothers of Jesus	Rom. 8:29; Heb. 2:11; Heb. 2:17
called by God	1 Thess. 5:24
chosen by God	1 Thess. 1:4
citizens of heaven	Phil. 3:20
clothed with Christ	Gal. 3:27
forgiven of all his/her sins	Col. 2:13
His children	Luke 20:36; John 1:12; Rom. 8:16; 1 John 3:1
His heirs	Rom. 8:17; Gal. 3:29; Gal. 4:7; Titus 3:7
His gift to Christ	John 10:29
His righteousness	2 Cor. 5:21

His sons	Gal. 3:26; Gal. 4:5
holy and blameless	Eph. 1:4
holy, without blemish, free from accusation	Col. 1:22
justified	Rom. 3:24
made perfect	Heb. 10:14
members of His household	Eph. 2:19
objects of Christ's intercession	Heb. 7:25

It is easy to see the powerful effect receiving such truths will have on the life of a Believer. It is important to remember that these truths are the Word of God and are, therefore, indisputable – and they apply to *every* Believer. What joy is available for the Christian who can see themselves as God sees them; for example, holy, without blemish and free from accusation (Col. 1:22). What a revolution will take place in the Believer's relationship with God when such a truth is accepted. What lightness of spirit is there for the Believer who can receive the truth that he or she is seen by God as holy and blameless (Eph. 1:4). And what glory to so great a God who has chosen to see His people in that way, and who gave His Son in order to make it possible.

Still more *Good* News – God's provision for the Believer

Every Believer has their every need provided for by God (Phil. 4:19). The provision includes:

the protection of God's Name	John 17:11
every spiritual blessing	Eph. 1:3
fullness in Christ	Col. 2:10
God's armour	Eph. 6:13-18
power to overcome the enemy	Luke 10:19
weapons with Divine power	2 Cor. 10:4

Summary

These are only a selection of many more such Scriptures. In Christ, and in essence, God says of each and every individual Believer, 'YOU are My son' whom I love; with YOU I am well pleased.' (Mark 1:11 author's emphasis). Let every Christian receive it, believe it and live it (Proverbs 23:7 *NKJV*), for that is the Word of God.

CHAPTER 13

'... as of first importance...'

Introduction
Sunday after Sunday, Bible study group after Bible study group, countless Christians hear messages preached and taught throughout the year, year after year. It would be easy to get the impression, with this apparent need to receive endless teaching and instruction, that the Gospel of Christ is quite complicated. There is a myriad of peripheral issues that Christians can debate indefinitely, and upon which they have a Biblically-given freedom to hold their own viewpoint. Is infant baptism valid or not? Is it right to have women priests? When a person dies, does he go straight to heaven or fall asleep until Christ returns? Is it right for a divorced person to seek remarriage in a church? Is there ever a case for abortion? Doctrinal issues and day to day issues eat away at the unity of the church. People leave a church in search of another. Some leave and drop out of fellowship all together. New groups are formed. Confusion and disunity abound. The outside world looks on at a church unable to love itself, let alone outsiders.

The Apostle Paul, in 1 Corinthians 15:1-11, outlines the things which are 'of first importance' to the Christian, as individuals and as a church. It is upon the issues which Paul covers in this passage in 1 Corinthians that there is no room for personal opinion. There is a need to hold to clear Biblical revelation and, as a church, to unite around that revelation. It is upon the issues revealed in this passage that Christians should know what they believe and why they believe those things. The issues that Paul labels in 1 Corinthians 15 as being 'of first importance' are the very basics of the Christian faith. If the church will only take hold of them, preach them and teach them, then far greater unity will be the result, a greater ability to evangelize will result, and Sunday morning services can concentrate on exalting the God who gave

Himself for mankind, rather than on the perennial search for a new angle on a 2,000 year old, very simple story.

'... as of first importance...'

In the passage 1 Corinthians 15:1-11 there are **six doctrinal issues** which Paul raises. They are:
i.   '... according to the Scriptures...' (verses 3 and 4) - doctrine must rest on **Biblical revelation**
ii. '... Christ died for our sins...' (verse 3) - *forgiveness* of sins through Christ's death;
iii. '... raised on the third day...' (verse 4) - Christian *justification*;
iv. '... He appeared to...' (verse 5) - the **assurance** of faith;
v.   '... I... do not even deserve...' (verse 9) - **undeserved grace**;
vi. '... His grace... was not without effect...' (verse 10) - **empowering grace**.

Paul considers that of first importance for the Christian is the truth that all doctrine must rest on a Biblical base. Forgiveness of sins through Christ's death is the basis of a Christian's relationship with God and another foundational truth of the Christian faith. Christian justification is, Biblically, based upon the resurrection of Christ and this is a third foundational truth of Christianity. It is so right that Paul highlights the Word of God, the cross and the empty tomb as the first three foundations of Christianity. Based upon these, Paul then highlights Christ's many post-resurrection appearances as a way by which Christians may have an assurance of what they believe. Paul then declares, as a foundational truth, that the grace extended by God to man is entirely undeserved, but goes on to point out, as the last foundational truth of Christianity, that receiving grace is the way to empowerment within the life of a Christian.

'... according to the Scriptures...'

If something is repeated in Scripture it is because it is considered, by God, to be of particular significance. The phrase '... according to the Scriptures...' is repeated in this passage and, therefore, it can be accepted that God considers this a point of particular significance. It is important for Christians to understand that Christ's life, death and resurrection were all in fulfilment of Scripture. God's plan for the salvation of mankind, through His Son, is outlined in Scripture from Genesis chapter 3 onwards. In Luke 24:27, when the post-resurrection Jesus was on the Emmaus road with two disciples, He explained to them all the events that had just occurred, involving Himself in Jerusalem 'beginning with Moses and all the Prophets.' The early disciples certainly knew the importance of a faith that rested on Biblical revelation, rather than only on experience or someone else's teaching. In Acts 17 is the account of the Apostle Paul in Thessalonica. He went to the synagogue and, with the Jews there, he (verses 2-3), '... reasoned with them from the Scriptures, explaining and proving that the Christ had to suffer and rise from the dead.' Another example of this Scriptural foundation for faith is in Acts chapter 8 when Philip explains the Good News about Jesus to the Ethiopian eunuch. In Acts 18:28 it tells of Apollos, an early convert who, '... vigorously refuted the Jews in public debate, proving from the Scriptures that Jesus was the Christ.' Jesus repeatedly told His disciples and others that His life, death and resurrection was to be in accordance with Scripture (Matt. 26:54. Mark 14:49, John 5:39 and others). It should be the desire of every Christian to so understand Scripture that when faced with false teaching, so prevalent today, that challenges the basics of the Christian faith - the virgin birth, the bodily resurrection of Jesus, the assurance of salvation and a many other fundamental issues - the Christian will be able, as Apollos, to vigorously refute the false teaching, proving from the Scriptures that Jesus is the Christ. A better understanding of the Scriptural revelation of salvation will strengthen each Christian's understanding of how salvation is entirely a work of God for man and, thus, clear up much of the confusion that exists today about man's role in his salvation. The need for such Scriptural knowledge is a foundational truth of the Christian faith.

'... Christ died for our sins ... '

This is the second foundational truth of the Christian faith which Paul lists as being 'of first importance.' Two thousand years after

"WHATEVER HAPPENED TO THE GOOD NEWS?"

Christ's death and resurrection there is a great deal of confusion within the Christian Church about how and when a Christian's sins are dealt with. This confusion adversely affects the day to day relationship which many Christians have with God. Within the Church today there are those who are expecting to be judged when they meet with God at the end of their time on earth. There are those, Christians, who have an underlying nervousness, even fear, at the thought of that encounter with God. The Catholic church has come up with the doctrine of purgatory which specifically lays the punishment for some of their sins upon the Catholic individual. Some born again Christians believe that God is less pleased with them, less close to them, less likely to bless them after they have sinned. Many Christians believe that their sins are dealt with by God as and when they occur and as forgiveness is requested. Yet the Scriptures say, 'Christ died for our sins.' Isaiah 53 makes it quite clear that Christ bore the sins of every person into Himself and, also, bore the punishment for those sins. This truth is the very basis of the Good News but it has become obscured by wrong teaching and, in Paul's day as now, there is a need to clearly proclaim the Good News that 'Christ died for our sins.' When John the Baptist saw Jesus he declared, 'Look, the Lamb of God who takes away the sin of the world' (John 1:29). Jesus Christ has taken away the sin of not only the Christian, but of everyone in the world (1 John 2:2). The only issue outstanding between God and mankind is acceptance or rejection of His Son (John 3:18 and others). Yet so many are still taught that their sin is an issue between them and God. Bible teachers get their listeners to go through such antics as writing their 'sins' on a piece of paper and then putting them into a bin as though this symbolized getting rid of the sin; another role-play is to write the troublesome 'sin' on a balloon and then release the balloon into the air – again symbolizing the going away of that sin. This dangerous form of teaching, which is quite widespread in its various forms, is in error in three major areas; firstly, it suggests that sin is still an issue between God and man – contrary to the revelation of Scripture; secondly, sin has still to be dealt with as it occurs – again, contrary to Scripture and, thirdly, it suggests that man himself plays some part in getting rid of his sin, which is also contrary to Scripture. It may seem a harmless exercise to go through such a role-play, but it is undermining the most basic truth of the Christian faith, that 'Christ died for our sins.' The Good News of the Gospel is that Christ died for our sins while we were still sinners (Romans 5:8). God did not wait for man to make every effort against sin before He made man acceptable to Himself through Christ. Equally, now the Christian has been made acceptable, God makes no demand that the Christian make every effort against sin, and so take on a heavy burden (contrary to Matt. 11:30) – because He Himself has dealt with man's sins. Romans 6:10 confirms that Jesus, when He died for our sins, 'died to sin once for all...' Jesus died once and He died for all. Let the Christian rejoice at the Good News, that 'Christ died for our sins' and in so doing dealt with sin for all time for all people. Let every Christian be assured that forgiveness of sins comes through the death of Christ, and the death of Christ alone. It cannot be added to, or taken away from. The Christian stands forgiven because, 'Christ died for our sins.'

'... raised on the third day ... '

Paul goes on to write, in the passage being examined, that Jesus, '... was raised on the third day according to the Scriptures...' In Romans 4:25 it says of Jesus that, 'He was delivered over to death for our sins and was raised to life for our justification.' The death of Christ, taking away all sin from the Believer, lays the foundation for a new relationship with God. The resurrection of Christ, assuring the Believer's justification, maintains an on-going relationship with God. Justification moves the Christian into the position of being as though he had never sinned. Once again Paul makes the point that this happened according to the Scriptures. Psalm 16:10, amongst others, contains a prophecy that Christ would rise from the dead. Paul quotes that particular Scripture in Pisidian Antioch, in Acts 13, and Peter refers to it in his address at Pentecost in Acts 2. The very exciting and Good News about the resurrection, apart from the fact that it means justification for the Christian, is that – as this is the means of Christian justification – it puts the responsibility for Christian justification squarely onto

God. So far in this passage Paul has revealed, through foundational truths of the Christian faith, that doing away with sin is entirely God's responsibility and justification of the Christian is, also, entirely God's responsibility. This is the very Good News of the Gospel. It allows no room for the doubts and fears that assail so many Christians through lack of knowledge of the basics of their faith. Romans 5:18 again points the Christian to Christ as his means of justification. It says, '... the result of one act of righteousness was justification that brings life for all men.' The Scriptures speak repeatedly (Rom. 3:24, 3:26, 5:1, 5:18, 1 Cor. 6:11, Gal. 3:24, Titus 3:7 amongst others) of how the Christian is justified by grace, through faith. Sending Jesus to bear the punishment due for sin was God's act of grace to man. The Christian's faith in Christ's resurrection provides for his justification. This means the day to day position of the Christian before God is entirely unaffected by the daily living of that Christian - and that's Good News!

'... He appeared to ...'

Christianity is not a religion of blind faith. In Acts 1:3 it says that after His resurrection Jesus appeared to His followers 'and gave many convincing proofs that He was alive.' Amongst the convincing proofs are His appearances, as listed in 1 Corinthians 15, to Peter, then the twelve apostles, then to a gathering of more than five hundred of His followers, then to James, then to all the apostles and, finally, to Paul. These appearances, excluding that to Paul, took place over a period of forty days. They occurred in different places and involved hundreds of different people. During the appearances Jesus gave other proofs that He was alive. In Luke 24:39 He invited the frightened disciples, who thought they were seeing a ghost, to touch Him and to feel His flesh and bone. He invited them to look at the wounds He carries from the crucifixion. He then ate some food with them to further prove that He was alive and not just an apparition. When Jesus appeared to the disciples on another occasion (John 20:27) He invited Thomas to touch the nail marks in His hand and to put his hand into the spear wound in Jesus' side.

Christianity is a religion that rests very much upon firm evidence. Many people have set out, through the years, to disprove Christianity; but, as an American lawyer discovered when he tried to disprove Christianity, there is enough evidence to prove in any fair court of law that Jesus Christ is exactly who He claimed to be. Christians are not supposed to live with doubts about the basics of their faith. Hebrews 10:22 encourages Believers to '... draw near to God with a sincere heart in full assurance of faith.' Full assurance! Any Believer having doubts should confront the doubts, following the example of Scripture. Many times people came to Jesus with their doubts: Satan said to Jesus, *'If* you are the Son of God...'; a leper came to Him and said, *'If* you are willing...'; Peter said to Jesus, when He was walking on water, *'If* it is You...' it is not wrong to have doubts, but it is foolish to live with those doubts rather than confronting them.

Christians are encouraged to live, knowing the many convincing proofs that Jesus gave to His followers – and still gives today to His followers, in full assurance of their faith. This is not a side issue, it should be remembered that it is one of the truths which is of first importance. A Christian with doubts is a far less effective witness than the Christian who does have that full assurance of faith.

'... I ... do not even deserve ...'

Paul recognised, and freely confessed, that he did not deserve to be called an apostle. He was one of the main persecutors of the fledgling Christian church. He calls himself, 'the least of the apostles.' Paul, though, does not stop with this confession of unworthiness. He goes on to say, 'But by the grace of God I am what I am.' This is the same attitude shown by the Prodigal Son, in Luke 15, when he returns home and is offered the undeserved love of the father he has wronged. In verse 21 of that chapter the son says, 'Father, I have sinned against heaven and against you. I am no longer worthy to be called your son.' Having recognised, and confessed, his unworthiness the son then goes on to receive the gifts of love, and the restoration to the position of sonship, which the father freely offers him. Both Paul and the Prodigal Son are demonstrating an important principle of grace, which is that it is extended to those who are undeserving and that to receive it is a positive choice made by the recipient.

This is the situation in which every human being finds him or herself. No-one is worthy of the gracious gift of Jesus and all that flows through Him. Every Christian, though, needs to adopt the same position as Paul and to be saying, 'I do not even deserve . . . but . . .' For example, 'I do not even deserve to be called a child of God, but by the grace of God I am what I am.' The recognition of the fact that no-one deserves grace then allows the Believer to choose to receive that grace – and that is what ensures that it remains grace. It will stop the Believer falling into the trap of striving to, in some way, be worthy of the mighty gift of Jesus and all the grace that flows through Him. Grace is extended by God to mankind without regard to conditions or response. Paul understood that, received grace and went on to serve the Gospel in a mighty way. This truth, of undeserved grace, is very rightly included in those that Paul considers to be of first importance. Two great problems weaken the Christian church today, and both are covered by Paul's listing of the truths of first importance. The first great weakness from which the modern church suffers is that the majority of Christian do not really know the Scriptures. They may be read, listened to and even learned; but there is a great lack of study and understanding – hence, superficial, traditional and even incorrect interpretations are accepted. The second great weakness of the Christian church today is its inability to accept God's freely offered grace. Bible teacher after Bible teacher, preacher after preacher, will encourage Christians to hold back from embracing grace in all its fullness, for fear that it may lead to licence. Yet, in the verse under discussion, Paul declares that it is the grace he has received which makes him the person he is; and it is the receiving of grace that makes every Believer today the person they are. Believers are called in the Scriptures children of God, brothers of Jesus, ambassadors of Christ and many other glorious names – none of them are deserved. All are positions freely offered.

'... His grace ... was not without effect'

Paul received grace which, although he didn't deserve it, was freely offered to him – as it is to every Believer and, indeed, every human being. Paul goes on in this passage to write that in the receiving of grace he was empowered to work harder than any of the others in the church. Paul is teaching here a truth 'as of first importance' that is, sadly, not understood by most Christians today and, indeed, is mistaught by the majority of Christian leaders, speakers, preachers and teachers. The truth is that, far from being an easy option or an alternative to obedience, grace is the very source of empowerment, service and obedience within the life of a Christian. It was not himself, declares Paul, but grace within him that produced all the hard work. What a great day for the church when Christians stop trying to do so much for God and allow God, 'who works in you to will and act according to His good purpose' (Phil. 2:13), to freely have His way. Colossians 1:6 tells what will happen in such an event. 'All over the world this gospel is bearing fruit and growing, just as it has been doing among you since the day you heard it and understood God's grace in all its truth.' Gospel growth and fruit bearing is assured – once the Christian understands grace. This is because that Christian will then be in the position of Paul and will allow grace to produce hard work for the Gospel – rather than striving do produce such work in human strength. Receiving grace also empowers personal growth. Romans 5:17 says, '... how much more will those who receive God's abundant provision of grace and of His gift of righteousness reign in life through the one man, Jesus Christ.' Receiving grace will empower the Christian to the point where he or she will reign in life – that is the Word of God. Grace is only ever taught in the Scriptures in the context of being a source of empowerment. How far these truths are from the fearful modern teaching that links abundant grace with descent into licence. Those who teach that Christians should beware of abusing grace, or should hold back from embracing grace 'too much,' demonstrate by such teaching their lack of understanding of the Bible's teaching on the matter. Let every Christian embrace grace wholeheartedly and let such Christians know the empowerment that grace brings. Let every

Christian declare to Believer and non-believer alike, 'By the grace of God, I am what I am.'

Conclusion

When the Apostle Paul preached the Gospel he did so, according to his testimony in 1 Corinthians 1:17, '... not with words of human wisdom, lest the cross of Christ be emptied of its power.' Paul did this because, as he said earlier in the same verse, that is what Jesus sent him to do. Christians have been blessed with a Gospel that is not only Good News, but is also very simple to understand. There may be a myriad of peripheral issues, but at the heart of the Gospel there are just six foundational truths which every Christian should know and live by.

The truths of the Christian Gospel which the Bible declares to be 'of first importance' are:

i. That all that is revealed in the life, death and resurrection of Christ happened according to the Scriptures;

ii. That sin has been dealt with, once for all, because Christ died for our sins that He might '*give* repentance and forgiveness of sins' to the Believer (Acts 5:31 author's emphasis);

iii. That Christ rose again on the third day and, by that, the Christian is forever justified;

iv. That Jesus '... gave many convincing proofs that He was alive' (Acts 1:3) and that, therefore, the Christian may have 'Full assurance of faith' (Heb. 10:22);

v. That grace is never deserved, and that to receive it or not is a choice made by each person;

vi. That grace is the source of power in a Christian's life – not an alternative to obedience.

This is the Gospel of Christ. This is the *Good* News!